To Chuck, Randy, Marty, Hawk, and Rich
for your service to protect our freedoms.

Flight of the Dragon Lady

Donald Pickinpaugh

Published by Donald Pickinpaugh, 2023.

While every precaution has been taken in the preparation of this book, the publisher assumes no responsibility for errors or omissions, or for damages resulting from the use of the information contained herein.

FLIGHT OF THE DRAGON LADY

First edition. June 28, 2023.

Copyright © 2023 Donald Pickinpaugh.

ISBN: 979-8223849278

Written by Donald Pickinpaugh.

Acknowledgments

I want to thank my wife for encouraging me to write all these stories. Without her, none of this would have happened. I would also like my mom and dad for all their encouragement over the years.

In addition, I need to thank Lt. Col Rick Bishop and Captain Brandon Jones for their help in the writing of this book. Cal Balsam, Mark Coultrap, and Anne Heskett for help in editing.

Introduction

What is it like to wrestle with a Dragon or dance with a Lady? This is the challenge all U-2 pilots must face when flying the Lockheed U-2 Dragon Lady.

When first seeing the aircraft, the plane resembles an awkward albatross bird from a prehistoric age. The Dragon Lady is always the most unique aircraft on any military ramp. She has 104 feet of wing span across her tiny fuselage. Two wheels make up her landing gear. Like a bicycle, one wheel is in the front and the other near the rear. Usually, the first question at airshows is, "How can the airplane stay upright on the runway?" Our only reply is, "You have to keep the wings level on landing, otherwise the Dragon will come alive."

The U-2 may not be pretty on terra firma, but she was never born to stay on the ground. In the air, the Dragon Lady has a whole new personality. She will climb to the heavens with no stops in between.

A little over 1,000 pilots have soared to the upper limits of our atmosphere alone in the U-2. All pilots have to make a reckoning with the Dragon, sooner or later. Hopefully, with experience, her occupants get to dance with the Lady more often than having to battle the Dragon.

This book describes our missions and what it is like to fly the most challenging aircraft in the United States Air Force. Grab your spacesuit and let's head out for an adventure of a lifetime.

The Dream to Fly

I stared at the ground and shook my head. Surrounded by 5,000 hogs, I wondered if this was all there was in life. Surely, there had to be something more for a kid from Northwest Kansas. The smell of hogs permeated from all of my being. I had not been on a date since I started working at the hog farm. Worst of all, I was not the boss and got stuck with all the nasty jobs.

I almost started to cry as I reflected on my current situation. I was tired of squirting toothpaste in my washing machine to get the hog smell out. I was unsure if the smell would ever leave my clothes or my nostrils.

One hog, in particular, wanted to eat me alive. It was a battle every day against that killer. I contemplated shooting that hog and having a barbeque feast. Temptation almost drove me to that extreme. A few months later the slaughterhouse would grant me that wish.

In the distance, I could hear a rumble from behind me. I spun around to see an enormous aircraft. It had eight engines attached to the wings. It had to be an Air Force B-52 on a low-level bombing run over the hog farm. I had never seen a B-52 before, and this one was barreling down on me.

As the plane flew overhead, I graciously waved to the crew. For a moment I thought they were waving back at me, or maybe they were just glad they were not in my shoes. The giant bomber left a trail of black smoke, disappearing beyond my visual range. Something in my life needed to change and I knew those pilots in that aircraft had the answer. I wanted to go and see the world, even if it was on a low-level bombing run.

Later that night, I told my parents I wanted to join the Air Force and fly jets. I had to get out of the hog farming business. My dad smiled and agreed with me. Both of my parents were my biggest encouragers in life. They thought I should head to college first to get my degree. After all, you needed a college degree to fly jets in the Air Force.

The year before, I had received my pilot's license and had logged almost 200 hours. Soon afterward, I ran out of money. Making six dollars an hour at the hog farm did not buy much aviation fuel.

My banker offered to loan me $30,000 to get all my ratings. He thought if I obtained an instrument and commercial rating I might get hired at a small regional airliner. After some soul-searching, I could not bring myself to borrow that kind of money. I knew there was no way I could ever pay the bank off. I had to go a cheaper route so I decided to head off to college.

College and I had a tough time from the very start. Since my dad was a high school teacher, college should have been a breeze. My problem was, I was lazy and tried to game the system. After one year, the money ran dry again. I needed another plan.

Discussing my options with my parents, they thought it would be best if I joined the Air Force. I knew without a college degree, I could not fly jets and would have to start out enlisted. At least I could be around jets and maybe even work on one.

I said goodbye to all my buds that summer before leaving home. None of my close family or friends had been in the military, so this was going to be a new adventure for me. I had never seen an ocean and had barely been out of the state of Kansas. I had faith that my destiny lies somewhere out there in the wild blue yonder. It was a new chapter in my life, and I dove in head first.

The Air Force

The Air Force recruiter asked me what job I might be interested in. I had no idea. Since I could not go in as an officer, I told him to assign me something to do with planes or pilots. He gave me a large book with all the job openings in alphabetical order. I only made it to the job title of Aerospace Physiological Specialist and asked what they did. The recruiter told me they operated the altitude chambers and trained pilots. I thought about it briefly and said, "I'll take it."

Soon afterward, the Air Force informed me I was assigned to the Physiological Support Division (PSD) at Beale Air Force Base in Northern California. I had heard about California from watching TV shows, and I was excited to see it for myself.

I arrived for Basic Training at Lackland Air Force Base in San Antonio. We were greeted by a shouting Technical Instructor, or TI, as they called them. My old man never shouted at me like this young Air Force Staff Sergeant did. Before that first evening was over, I had learned a whole new vocabulary in the English language. I thought our instructor might kill all my classmates and me before we made it to bed.

The following week life in the Air Force started to settle down as we figured out what the military wanted from us. It boiled down to listening before speaking, marching in correct formation, and paying attention to detail. Once a person had the secret code down, Basic Training was a piece of cake.

My parents traveled down from Kansas for my graduation six weeks later. I could see they were proud of their young son. The Air Force was a giant step up from hog farming.

***

After graduation, I traveled across San Antonio to Brooks Air Force Base. I would accomplish my technical training in Aerospace

Physiology here. I enjoyed tech school as people were not yelling at us all the time. Our training now focused on learning a new job skill. The teachers treated us like adults, and I was slowly starting to enjoy this new lifestyle.

First, we set out to learn how to operate the altitude chambers. The large metal boxes were designed for the pilots to sit inside while all the air was taken out of the chamber. The lack of oxygen simulated a condition called hypoxia. We taught the pilots how to recognize their symptoms, and then how to recover from those symptoms. Any time a pilot was operating an Air Force aircraft, they needed to be on the lookout for hypoxia symptoms.

Once checked out in the altitude chamber, we were trained in the hyperbaric chamber. This chamber operated just the opposite of the altitude chamber. Now pressurized air was being forced into a metal tube. If a pilot suffered from a rapid decompression and had the bends, then they would have to go in this chamber. By forcing 100% oxygen into the body, the nitrogen levels in the bloodstream would be reduced. This could save a pilot's life so they could fly another day.

Six weeks later, I graduated from technical school and started my journey to my next destination, Beale Air Force Base, California. I had never ventured very far from the state of Kansas, and I could not wait to see the Pacific Ocean.

***

I picked up a new car in Kansas and started the long drive across the country. When I arrived at Beale, I was assigned to the training section of the Physiological Support Division (PSD). The building was divided into five sections: training, suits, oxygen, seat kits and parachutes, and operations. A new airman, like myself, had to complete each section before being fully qualified to launch a crewmember.

In the training section, we ran the same altitude chambers I had operated in San Antonio. It was a breeze, and I felt very comfortable at all the positions. We were also responsible for providing water survival training for all the pilots at a nearby lake. Water survival consisted of dressing the pilots up in their spacesuits and then dumping them into the water. Usually, we threw the parachute over the pilot as a simulation that might actually happen in a real ejection. The pilots would try to work their way to the side to free themselves of the chute. Once this was accomplished, the crewmembers had to be able to get into their one-person life raft. This was the most challenging part of the process, as the suit weighed 35 pounds. The trick was to get into the raft before the suit filled up with water. If a suit took on too much water, getting into the life raft was virtually impossible.

A few weeks later, John Young and Robert Crippen from NASA showed up to get their water survival training from us. They were scheduled to fly the first Space Shuttle mission in April. Both men stood out in their blue flight suits as we fitted them with a pair of SR-71 spacesuits. Both men were excited to be the first selected to take up the space shuttle. They were polite as we asked them many questions about their upcoming flight.

After two months in the training section, I moved on to the oxygen section. As I was walking down the hallway on my first day in the oxygen section, an African American man from Buffalo yelled, "Young man, get your eyes off of the floor and stand up tall."

I was surprised as this was the first time somebody had yelled at me since I had left Basic Training. I started laughing even though he outranked me by several stripes.

"Welcome to Oxygen," Staff Sergeant Glenwood Peterson said while laughing. Glenwood would be my mentor and best friend over the next three years. He taught me how to walk confidently and look people straight in the eye. Glenwood instilled confidence in me that I would use for the rest of my life. Still today, I remind myself of the life lessons he taught me.

The oxygen training mainly dealt with only two pieces of equipment, the helmet regulator and the suit controller. The dual helmet regulator provided 100% oxygen to the pilot's face mask at all times. The dual suit controller used ambient air to inflate the suit and ventilation for comfort.

The suit pressure controller consisted of two thin round diaphragms about three inches in diameter. If the controller sensed a loss of cabin pressurization, the diaphragms would automatically close all venting air and inflate the suit. This would ensure the pilot could survive a rapid decompression above the 70,000 feet they operated at. The crewmembers also had the ability to inflate the suit themselves to assist them in going to the bathroom.

Working in the Oxygen section was tedious and required an incredible amount of patience. The suit controllers needed a skilled hand to manipulate the diaphragms into place. Glenwood was the best and taught the rest of us the fine art of working with such small pieces of equipment.

Next, I was on to the Suit section. Each U-2 and SR-71 pilot had two suits and two outer garments containing the life preserver. In addition, the pilot had one helmet and a pair of boots. The suits were best described as balloons inside of a fish net. We could adjust the fish nets to any size to match a pilot's physical dimension.

My job in the Suit section was to preflight each suit for the pilots' upcoming missions and to postflight the suit after they landed. The tolerances for any leaks in a suit were so small that once inflated, it would take a month for a suit to run out of air.

After two months in Suits, I was assigned to the Seat Kits and Parachutes section. In this section, we made sure the batteries in the radios were all charged and performed regular inspections of all the survival equipment. The survival equipment was all located inside the seat kit, which weighed about 35 pounds. During an ejection, the pilot would only have what was in the seat kit to survive.

The parachute shop did the actual repack of the parachute, as we were not qualified for that part. I was glad; who would want to be responsible if a crewmember died because of a chute failure?

My final stop in my year-long training was Launch Operations. In this section, we were responsible for the entire phase of launching the U-2 or SR-71. The day before the launch we loaded the seat kit and parachute in the aircraft.

On the day of the launch, we would give the pilots a quick physical by checking their temperature and blood pressure. We also asked them a series of questions to ensure they were ready to go. At this time, the pilots would request what drinks and food they wanted on their flight. The "tube food," as we called it, was made by Gerbers, the same stuff we ate as babies. The various options include pears, peaches, and applesauce. A few choices were downright nasty, like Sloppy Joes and bacon and eggs. All of the tube food had "made by dates" before I was born. We calculated the food was good for decades, if not a lifetime, in its sealed tube.

Once the pilots had completed the physical, they would head into the dressing room. Here they put on their long johns with their urinary collection device, or UCD. For men, the UCD consisted of a giant condom, and women wore an elastic diaper. When stepping into the suit, both men and women would hook up their UCDs to a hose inside the suit. This enabled them to inflate the suit with airflow moving through the UCD to help urine exit. Though it was not a perfect design, it was the best we had at the time.

After the pilots were zipped up in the suit, we put on their outer garment and boots. Once they were dressed, I would run a series of leak checks on the suit to ensure everything fit nice and snug. The pilots had to pre-breathe 100% oxygen for an hour before they could launch. This would ensure that most of the nitrogen in the bloodstream was exhaled through their mouths so the crewmember would not get the bends while flying.

We then transported the pilots in a white box van to the aircraft and attached them to the seat kit and parachute in the aircraft. When the pilot was ready to close the canopy, we pulled four pins and a cover cap:

· The primary ejection pin
· The secondary ejection pin
· The scramble handle pin
· The parachute pin
· The drogue chute cover cap

We would show all the pins to the pilot and mobile backup pilot and get a thumbs-up sign. Once we were out of the way, the mobile pilot closed the canopy and it was showtime. The recovery procedure was just a reverse of the launch.

On one particular launch, I was suiting up Captain Rick Bishop. I'd always admired Rick as he drove a cool metallic gray 924 Porsche and was a fun guy at heart. He was well-liked by all the enlisted guys and gals and always took an interest in what we were doing. He asked me one day what I wanted to do after PSD. I told him someday I was going to fly the U-2. He smiled and encouraged me to go after that dream.

One day I was recovering an SR-71 pilot trainee. Due to the speed of the SR-71, the canopy railing would get extremely hot. All the qualified pilots knew to extend their arms over the hot railing to protect the PSD technician from getting burned. I waited for the trainee to extend his arms, but he did not understand what I wanted him to do, as he was enclosed in the spacesuit. Needing to install the pins, I decided not to wait for him and reached over the canopy rail. Immediately, I felt the intense burning sensation on my chin from the blistering hot canopy. The canopy fried my chin so bad it created a scar I would carry for the rest of my life. After watching me writhing in pain, the trainee pilot realized his mistake.

When I had completed all my training at PSD, my boss sent me on temporary duty assigned to Detachment 2 at Osan Air Base, South

Korea. We were on a two-month rotation. I went with one of my best friends, Bill Kyle.

During my time in Osan, Bill and I were on the recovery team. It was the best job in the world. We showed up at work thirty minutes before the U-2 was scheduled to land. We preflighted the primary and secondary pilot's pressure suits for the next day's mission and then postflighted the landing pilot's suit. All told we were at work for about 45 minutes each day.

It was a great time in Korea, except the cold winter was brutal. The weather reminded me of my home back in Kansas with the icy cold winds. I was ready to get back to California to warm up.

On my next deployment, I was sent to Detachment 1 at Kadena Air Base in Okinawa, Japan. It was the summer of 1982. My mentor Glenwood Peterson would join me for this tour. We launched the SR-71 or "Habu" as the locals called it to keep an eye on the North Koreans. Every once in a while the SR-71 would fly missions south of us to the South China Sea area.

Since the SR-71 did not fly every day as the U-2 did, we had plenty of time off to go snorkeling and see the sights on the island. I played tennis regularly with one Habu pilot named Major Les Dyer. He usually beat me in tennis, but on a rare occasion, would let me win.

For a small-town kid who grew up in Kansas, the weather in Okinawa was spectacular. It was a paradise, and we took full advantage of every moment to explore the island.

The two months I spent at Kadena AB went by fast. Before leaving, I started coordinating to return as soon as possible. My bosses back home were more than happy to accommodate my request. Three weeks later, I found myself back for another two months in paradise.

On one particular day, we launched an SR-71 scheduled to do a double loop, one track to the north and the other to the south of the base. After completion of the first track, the entire detachment gathered on the ramp to watch the SR-71 pass directly over the base, flying at 85,000 feet. This was exciting as none of us had ever seen an SR-71 except for takeoff and landings. When the aircraft was directly overhead, the pilot dumped a small amount of fuel so we could spot the aircraft. The aircraft was just a tiny speck in the bright blue sky and was only visible because of the fuel streaming behind the plane. A few seconds later, three soft sonic booms hit the ground. It was an amazing sight to see the world's fastest aircraft in action.

When I returned to Beale in the fall, I realized I needed to change jobs. I was enrolled in college classes, but the overseas deployments with PSD put a strain on the number of classes I could take. With no internet at the time, taking classes 4,000 miles away was not an option. I started to work on transferring into the Electronic Intelligence field. I chose this line of work because it paid a bonus, and I was always flat-broke and needed money.

My final deployment with PSD was to RAF Mildenhall in the United Kingdom. Both the U-2 and the SR-71 were stationed there. Our office had a larger number of enlisted crews, as some days we would have to launch both aircraft. One spy plane would head to the Baltic region in the north and the other to the south, providing constant surveillance on the Russians.

I spent Thanksgiving and Christmas in England in the winter of 1982. The sun hardly ever came out, so we were always in our winter parka gear. Even with several layers of clothing underneath our parka, I always felt frozen.

On New Year's Eve, my good friend Louie Tromboli and I headed to London to ring in the New Year in Trafalgar Square. As the sun set, we ducked into a pub only a few blocks from the Square to grab a bite to eat. The pub got packed quickly, and we decided it was time to get a better spot in the middle of the action.

We left the pub only to find ourselves in a solid wall of other revelers struggling to move in any direction. There had to be a million people in the center of London that night. Louie was a weightlifter, so I followed close behind him. We could only move a few inches at a time. As midnight approached, we only made it half a block closer to the Square. From our side street, we could not even see Big Ben as the clock struck midnight. It was useless, as we would spend that New Year's Eve on a side street only able to see the fireworks from a distance.

Once the fireworks stopped, the crowd started to disperse in our direction. It was a madhouse. One moment we were trying to go in one direction and the next we were being forced backward. We never did see Trafalgar Square that night.

The next morning, we jumped out of bed and headed to the Square. We were determined to at least see Big Ben. When we arrived at the square, articles of clothing were hanging off all the statues inside the fountains. We counted over a hundred pairs of shoes around the square. That New Year's Eve was the last time I spent in a crowd like that. I hated the helpless feeling of not being able to move. If I had not been behind my good buddy Louie, I probably would have been squashed.

The next summer Hollywood came to Beale. Our parking lot at PSD was packed with semi-trucks full of moving-making equipment. The movie was named, "Call to Glory." The main character was Craig T. Nelson playing a U-2 pilot. We were all excited, as we had never been on a movie set before. One afternoon, they asked for some volunteers to film a small part on the flightline. I anxiously volunteered. They asked all the volunteers to look up into the sky at a distressed U-2 coming in for a landing. We filmed several takes and then received $25 for our time and effort. The next year when the movie came out, I was excited to see my part. For some odd reason, they cut it out. My acting career had ended before it even started.

***

In the fall of 1983, I finally got accepted to be an Electronic Intelligence Analyst. I would be listening to the signals the U-2 and SR-71 collected on their missions.

The Air Force sent me to another technical school, this time for six months. I learned all about signal collection and identification. The school was located in Biloxi, Mississippi. We had to identify all the early warning and target tracking radars in the Russian inventory. As with most technical schools, the Air Force dragged the training process out way too long. After graduation, I was ready for my new assignment.

I was randomly picked to work at the National Security Agency (NSA) at Fort Meade, Maryland. I had never heard of this agency before being assigned there. I was looking forward to being stationed on the east coast, as I had never been to this part of the country before.

On my first day at work, I was amazed at how many people worked at the NSA. The parking lot resembled a college football game. If you were late, you had to park in the back forty and walk. That would add an extra ten minutes to your day each way. It was a massive facility.

I was assigned to an office on the second floor with several other Army tech sergeants. I quickly realized I was the stupidest person in the room. The two Army intelligence specialists were well beyond me in radar signal knowledge. My attitude toward the Army changed that day.

One of the Army techs was probably the smartest person on the planet in signal intelligence. On several occasions, our civilian bosses would bring in a tape for us to identify that had baffled other analysts. The Army tech would listen patiently, and then replay the tape while we all watched him in action. After the tape stopped the second time, he would reveal the Russians had a new radar signal. We were in awe of his talent. It was both impressive and sad at the same time. On one hand, it was amazing to watch a brilliant analyst in action. At the same time, we knew the military-industrial complex would never let this guy go. He was too valuable of a national asset for them to lose. They would find a way to keep him at the NSA for the rest of his career.

I applied to the University of Maryland School for Business within a few weeks of arrival. The admissions lady said all the business classes were full; was there was another major I wanted to study? I hadn't thought about it before and told her to pick one for me. She picked Political Science. That was fine with me. All I needed was a college degree to get into Officers School and then maybe Flight School.

My typical day consisted of eight hours of school, eight hours of work, and eight hours of sleep. That filled up my day for the next three years. I took as many courses as I could muster in those eight hours. After class, I would head to work for the swing shift.

My job was to take signals collected on reel-to-reel tapes and superimpose them onto print film. Everything was fairly automatic as the reel-to-reel tapes would rewind by themselves. Once all the signals were on the print film, I packed it up and sent it to whoever requested it. Every 30 minutes, I had to punch a button to reset the printer. I thought this was somewhat crazy, since I spent six months training to hit this button once every 30 minutes. The great part about this job was that in the other 29 minutes, I had the opportunity to type up all my Political Science reports. With so much time on my hands, I could knock out an entire class in a couple of work days.

I decided to take one class on Arab-Israeli relations. My teacher had a beard and worked for the Jerusalem Post newspaper. His name was Wolf Blitzer. Only five people were in our small class, so we had a good time discussing all the problems in the Middle East. I had no idea where most of those countries were located on a map. I definitely had no idea a few years later I would be flying over most of them.

Wolf was always curious about what I did at the NSA. I told him I punched a button every 30 minutes, which was the truth. I'm not sure he ever believed me.

Nearing graduation, I contacted Major Rick Bishop and Major Les Dyer to see if they would write me letters of recommendation for Officers School. They agreed, and I started my application process. I had to go to Andrews Air Force Base to get a flight physical to see if I met the qualifications for Flight School. After collecting all my paperwork, I submitted my package and waited anxiously for the answer.

A month later, I got a rejection letter. I was devastated. My 3.2 grade point average in Political Science was not competitive against my peers. My dream of Flight School and flying the U-2 was now down the drain. I didn't even have an alternate plan since I was so focused on Flight School.

It took me a few days to recover from the devastating news. The Army techs I worked with all had master's degrees and taught night classes at the local college. I thought it sounded like a good idea and started my master's application at Maryland. It didn't seem like too bad of an idea since my dad was also a school teacher. I never thought I would follow in his footsteps.

A month later, the Army Colonel held a squadron meeting outside, and I was told I needed to be there. At first, I thought I might be in trouble. Why would he want me there? I worked the swing shift and had no time to get into trouble. I was puzzled by the summons, but like a good airman, I followed orders and dusted off my uniform.

After several announcements, the Army Colonel called me up to the stage. I was shaking in my boots. I had no idea if this was my last day in the Air Force.

The Colonel turned to me and announced to the group, "Staff Sergeant Pickinpaugh just got accepted to Officer School."

I was shocked and thought something was wrong. I had been turned down a month earlier. The Colonel shook my hand as all my fellow workers clapped. I didn't know what to think. Surely a Colonel would not pull a prank on me like this.

When the Colonel finished, I said in a soft voice, "I think I was turned down for Officers School."

"You were," he replied. "But that was the first round. Any declines automatically go to a second board, and you got selected."

My mouth dropped as my heart pounded wildly in my chest. In less than a month, I had the most devastating news of my life along with the best news. That day was an emotional roller coaster, but now I was back on cloud nine.

The next day, I stopped at the military uniform store. I bought all new clothes along with Second Lieutenant Epaulets. I stood in front of the mirror taking it all in. I had a mustache, and officers didn't have mustaches. I shaved it off right then.

***

I showed up to Officers School with a new spring in my step. Captain Lim was my Flight Instructor. She was a Korean-American lady who taught us all how to become good officers in the Air Force. I already knew the marching part and was prepared for the twelve-week course. Officer School was more formal than my Basic Training six years earlier. In Basic Training, they yelled you into submission. In Officers School, they wanted you to use your head to figure out solutions to problems.

Shortly after arriving at Officers School, the Space Shuttle Challenger exploded on liftoff. It was a horrific sight to watch and a tough day for America. My first thought went to Young and Crippen when I gave them water survival training at Beale. Was either of them on that flight? A short time later, I found out they were not on that mission. Even though I was grateful, other families had just lost their loved ones. All the flights in Officers School stood in formation that evening. The band played taps as we lowered the American flag. Tears rolled down everyone's faces. It was a day we would never forget.

Officers School was drawing to a close. I excelled in math, history, and science at school. However, English was always my Achilles heel. The written language made my head hurt. I mean, what good is an adverb anyway? It probably didn't help that I always skipped Mr. Brooks's English class in High School.

I had the lowest possible English grade to pass Officers School, but it was just good enough. I received great scores in all the other subjects. If only those hogs could have helped me with my English.

After 90 days, I graduated from Officers School. My parents were in attendance again. They were troopers.

I left San Antonio and headed north to Lubbock, Texas. Lubbock was home to Reese Air Force Base. The flat terrain of North Texas was a perfect place to learn how to fly Air Force jets. It will be my home for the next year.

One Dream Fulfilled

Soon after arriving on base, I went to the uniform store and picked up a couple of flight suits. I was back in front of a mirror, inspecting my green uniform. It was light and very comfortable to wear. The flight suit felt so good, I didn't want to take it off. I took out an old black U-2 pin I had held on to since my days at PSD and pinned it on my lapel. One step closer to flying the Dragon Lady, I reminded myself.

I showed up the next day for Flight School at 8 am. There were a total of 29 other students in my class. Captain Brad Arnold, our Flight Commander, told us that half of us would be gone within the year. Yikes, I thought. That was a high attrition rate. Our commander was not too far off. We started with 30 students and graduated 19 in my flight.

After my commander's speech, I met my new instructor, Captain Domenic Eanniello. He immediately asked me what the black pin on my lapel was while reminding me I was out of uniform. I started to get a little nervous and didn't know how to react. I did not want to start off flight school on the wrong foot. I graciously informed him it was a U-2 pin. I told him I had previously suited up U-2 and SR-71 pilots and wanted to fly the U-2. He smiled and told me he was leaving in two weeks to go fly the Dragon Lady. We would laugh about that moment over the years.

The T-37 program was fun and exciting. Within 13 hours, we were soloing in a twin-engine jet. I felt comfortable because of my previous hours of flying little civilian airplanes. Still, the T-37 was a handful, as the jet sped along the ground at twice the speed I was accustomed to. During my time in the T-37, I met one of my best friends. His name was Second Lieutenant Tom Ruggerio. Tom came from New Jersey and was an aerospace engineer at Georgia Tech. He was the smartest person I had ever come across, with his photographic memory. During our entire year at Flight School, Tom only missed two questions out of

1500. All of my fellow students knew we could count on Tom to help us understand some of the more difficult subjects.

The day before Independence Day 1986, I was flying with my instructor and lined up on 17L at Reese to land. Out of the corner of my eye, I could see smoke coming from the center runway, slightly off to the right of the runway I was going to land on. I knew immediately there was a problem and figured an airplane had just crashed. I couldn't stare too long or otherwise I would mess up my landing. Soon the fire trucks were rolling as we taxied back into our parking spot. I always knew military flying was not without risk, but I had just seen it firsthand. Later that day, we heard a T-38 female instructor pilot had died.

After several checkrides, we completed T-37s and moved on to the faster T-38. This aircraft could go twice as fast as the T-37. One flight in the T-38 was called the "Boom Ride." Our instructor took us up to 40,000 feet and then dove toward the ground while passing the speed of sound. The airspeed indicator in the cockpit read just above Mach 1.0, letting us know we were supersonic. This was a new experience as none of us students had ever flown faster than the speed of sound before.

In T-38s, one of my instructors was First Lieutenant Jeff Gruver. He would also go on to fly the U-2 a year later. I loved flying with Jeff as he was an old-school stick and rudder pilot. He was the kind of man that would give you the shirt off his back.

I graduated from flight school in the middle of the pack. Over the long year, we lost almost half of our classmates, so I felt good about graduating. Flight School was one of the hardest things I had ever done, and along with it came the reward of being an Air Force pilot.

During our assignment ceremony, we had to spin a big wheel with various names of Air Force aircraft around the outside. Wherever the wheel stopped, that would be our assigned airplane. My classmates reserved one of the spots on the wheel for a U-2. The U-2 was the only aircraft a student could not get assigned to right out of Flight School. The U-2 program required at least 1,000 hours of instructor time or 1,500 hours as an aircraft commander. I had neither. When the wheel stopped spinning, it landed on the T-37. That was fine with me, as I figured it was the fastest way to get the hours required to fly the U-2. My good friend Tom Ruggiero was also assigned the T-37 with me.

Once we graduated, both Tom and I headed off to San Antonio for Pilot Instructor Training. The course was 90 days long and taught us how to train student pilots. We had a blast as this course was a gentlemen's program. The one tricky part was looking across the cockpit at the student's instrument gauges. The instructor did not have any gauges so we had to glance across the cockpit to see their gauges. After a few flights, both Tom and I started to feel comfortable in our new instructor roles.

After Instructor School, we returned to Reese to start three years as T-37 Instructor Pilots. Both Tom and I were initially assigned to Charlie Flight as instructors.

When my first students showed up I was as nervous as they were, but I tried not to show it. I was now responsible for teaching this brand-new Second Lieutenant how to fly. A year earlier, I was in their shoes, and now I was in charge. Soon, my military training took over, and I developed my own teaching techniques.

Two weeks went by and I soloed my first student. After a student soloed, the rest of their classmates would throw the student into a horse trough full of water. It was a rite of passage. When an Instructor Pilot soloed their first student, they got the same treatment. The students found me first and tossed me head-first into the water. It was the middle of December and the unrecognizable top layer of the water had frozen over. As my hand hit the ice, parts of it broke off and jabbed me above my right eye. Blood gushed out of my forehead as the water started to turn red. All the students gasped in horror at the sight of blood everywhere. They quickly surmised they were in hot water. I was soon off to the hospital for a dozen stitches and no worse for the wear. After the dunk tank episode, everybody called me "Icepick." That nickname became my new callsign and stuck with me for the remainder of my career.

Two of my first students would become a couple of my best friends over my life, Second Lieutenants Cal Balsam and Mark Coultrap. They were both sharp as a whip and easy to train. Tom and I liked them so much that we brought both of them back to be instructors. Eventually, down the road, we would all work together at the same airline. It was a small world.

Another one of my students was Second Lieutenant Dave Rand. His dad had flown U-2s as part of the original CIA pilots, which included the famous Gary Powers. I was fascinated by all the stories Dave recited to me about growing up around all the U-2 pilots. I tried to talk him into eventually flying the U-2, as I thought it would be a great idea to have a father and son fly the Dragon Lady. Instead, Dave had his heart set on flying the big C-5 cargo plane. Dave did get his C-5 to Travis Air Force Base on assignment night. It was good to see him accomplish his dream.

Nearing the end of my tour at Reese, I would get assigned students having difficulties. Most senior instructors would have one or two students that required more time and effort to train. I always thought I could train anybody to fly, but flight school had specific standards that had to be met by a certain number of flights. If a student did not meet those standards, then the Air Force cut them from the flying program.

One student, Second Lieutenant Dave Morelock, was struggling through the T-37 program. Dave and I were assigned a cross-country flight on a long weekend. We took off for Colorado Springs to practice some instrument approaches. This involved the students positioning their helmet visor covers so they could not see outside of the cockpit. This training simulated being in the clouds in a real-world environment, so the students had to rely only on their instrument gauges.

Dave had numerous problems on the first leg as he kept losing his situational awareness. I felt sorry for him because it is not easy to fly a jet with only the gauges in your cockpit for reference. That evening, as the rest of our gang went out on the town, Dave and I stayed behind in our hotel rooms. We spent long hours reviewing the basics of flying in the weather. I would walk around the room with a model airplane in my hand as Dave looked at a blowup chart of our cockpit instruments. It was a long and tedious evening, but in the end, I thought Dave started to understand the concept of instrument flying.

The next day we headed toward Amarillo, Texas. I had Dave put his visor cover on as soon as we were airborne. I encouraged him without helping him navigate his way to Amarillo. Upon arrival, we shot two instrument approaches, and Dave did an excellent job.

When we landed, I gave Dave an Excellent on his grade sheet. It was the first time he had received an excellent grade in pilot training. I had never seen a student pilot so excited. He was full of confidence, and I couldn't have been more proud of him. His expressions and happiness were the greatest honors an instructor pilot can achieve.

Seven years later, Khobar Towers in Dhahran, Saudi Arabia; was blown up by a terrorist, killing nineteen American airmen. Captain Dave Morelock was in the building. He miraculously survived with bruises and cuts to his face. I was in the auditorium when President Clinton presented Dave with the Purple Heart while presiding over the funeral of five of his fellow airmen. It was one of the proudest moments in my Air Force career and also one of the saddest.

A few months later, I hit the 1,000-hour time as an instructor pilot. I immediately sent in my application to the U-2 program. Lieutenant Colonel Bill Gilbert called me a week later to say they would offer me an interview. I was on cloud nine and could not hold back the tears. It had taken seven long years to get the opportunity of a lifetime. I had one last step to go. I had to pass the interview.

The U-2 Interview and my other Dream

I walked into the 99th Reconnaissance Squadron at the end of April 1990. The interview process consisted of five interviews with various commanders from each of the two squadrons, wing staff, and the Wing Commander.

My first interview was with the Commander of the 99th RS, Lt. Col. Rick Bishop. Yes, the same pilot who wrote me a letter of recommendation years earlier to get into Officers School. He had moved up two ranks since I last saw him. It was good to see Rick after seven long years. We had both changed a lot. I felt some pressure as I did not want to disappoint him, but I would give it my best shot.

During most U-2 interviews, the Commanders asked the interviewees why they wanted to fly the U-2. I did not get that question, as Rick already knew the answer. Rick looked me straight in the eye and said, "If you can't fly the plane, I can't hire you."

"Fair enough," I replied. "I just want the same chance everybody else gets." I respected him for his honesty.

My following interview was with Lt. Col. Bruce Cucuel, the Commander of the 5th SRTS. Bruce was another pilot I remembered from my days at PSD. He told me the same thing as Rick. I needed to perform, or they would have to let me go.

The second part of the interview was to see if I could actually fly the Dragon Lady. We would stay close to the runway and practice landing the beast.

The next day, I jumped into the backseat of a two-seat U-2 used for training. The taxi wheels, or "Pogos" as everybody called them, would stay with me on my first flight. Typically, the Pogos would fall off during takeoff, but for the first flight with an interviewee, the outrigger type wheels were left attached. Probably for the best, as the Dragon could bite faster than most instructors could recover the aircraft.

Rick demonstrated the first takeoff. The U-2, with its light load, lifted off in only 300 feet and was at 5,000 feet in 20 seconds. My jaw dropped as I was in total awe of the Dragon Lady's performance. Nothing I had ever flown could match this performance.

Rick demonstrated the first two landings as I followed along on the controls. I tried to mimic his every movement while he was landing the aircraft.

The Dragon Lady was a handful, but everything I had dreamed of. Unlike all the other aircraft in the Air Force inventory, the U-2 had to be stalled out a couple of feet above the runway. Stalling any other aircraft while airborne would be a mistake and lead to a bad day. But not the U-2; it was designed to be stalled during which time the plane would stop flying and land tailwheel first.

Sweat was raining down my facemask as I tried to see out the front of the cockpit. The Dragon Lady did not provide any comforts like air conditioning to its victims.

Rick would yell, "Raise your left-wing, raise your right-wing, more left rudder," and so on.

It seemed like I could not get anything right at first on my landings. I not only had to stall the plane, but I also had to keep the wings level at the same time. Slowly I picked up on the slight variations in the tilt of the aircraft to keep my wings level. It was like sitting in the middle of a teeter-totter and trying to balance both ends of the wooden plank. I was overloaded, to say the least.

I also had to keep the plane going straight down the centerline after each landing. Then after I was somewhat stable, I had to reset the trim, raise the flaps, and advance the throttle for another takeoff. We did multiple touch-and-goes on that first flight.

My right arm was throbbing and shaking when we pulled into the chocks. I was soaked from head to toe. As I took my helmet off, sweat poured out. I had never felt so beaten up in my life. Now, I had even more admiration for the Dragon Lady pilots.

Some interviewees called it a day after the first ride, while PSD would help them out of the aircraft. They realized the Dragon Lady was not for them. That was not going to be me. My body ached with pain as I climbed down the stairs. I remember what Glenwood Peterson said about always holding my head high. Even if Rick fired me, I had gotten to fly the U-2 at least once. I had accomplished part of my dream.

During the debrief, Rick reiterated that my landings needed work. I expected he would say as much, as it was probably the same speech all U-2 interviewees get after their first flight. He told me they wanted to see improvement over the next two flights.

That night I returned to my quarters and took a long hot shower. My body was still in pain. I wondered how in the world the Dragon Lady pilots did it every day.

On the next flight, Rick had maintenance remove the attachment pins from the pogos so that they would fall free during takeoff. I knew that was a good sign since Rick had some confidence in my abilities to land the aircraft. We continued flying around the pattern, practicing simulated flameout landings and no-flap landings. I was gaining more confidence in myself as my landings showed some improvements.

The next day, I flew with Lt. Col. Ken Tupper. Ken was a soft-spoken man and had me correct some little mistakes. I finally started to use the elevator trim, which took some workload off my sore right arm. Taxiing into our parking spot after my third flight, I took a deep breath. I thought I did okay, but I did not know for sure. What was the standard they were looking for? I had no idea.

I sat in my soaking wet flight suit as Rick and Ken talked for the longest ten minutes of my life. I could feel the pressure in my chest, ready to explode.

Soon the door opened, and Rick motioned for me to enter. I looked for clues on his face, but there were none to be found. He turned to me and said, "Congratulations, you are the newest U-2 pilot."

I had done it. I didn't know whether to cry or to hug him. It was a long road. It was my 29th birthday. It was the greatest birthday gift I would ever receive.

Rick could tell I was ecstatic, but he wasn't going to let me get a big head just yet. "You still have to get through training," he responded.

I nodded and thanked them both.

A few months later, I rented a U-Haul and pulled my old white Porsche on a trailer behind it. Tom and Cal helped me move out to California. I was going to be a U-2 pilot with a Porsche, just like Lt. Col. Rick Bishop.

When I arrived at Beale, Chuck Cunningham, my old friend from my instructing days at Reese, let me live with him. Chuck was easygoing, and we had a blast. He was in several U-2 training classes in front of me. His training partner was Captain Troy Devine. Troy was a former T-38 instructor at Williams Air Force Base in Arizona. She was the first female to get accepted into the U-2 program. Troy was a competitor. If we went water skiing, she had to beat the boys. If we went trap shooting, Troy would beat us all. She did not know what second place was. It was not in her vocabulary.

Even though Troy lived forty miles away, she was always at Chuck's house. Sometimes they studied together; sometimes, they just hung out. Right off the bat, I knew that they were all giddy about each other. A few years later, they got married, a first in the U2 program.

When I showed up to work in my Porsche, I soon learned Rick Bishop no longer had his old Porsche. He had sold it years earlier and now had a BMW. I was disappointed; there was no way in the world I was going to get a BMW. What kind of U-2 pilot would drive a BMW?

My training at Beale started with the T-38 program. It had been three years since I last flew the T-38, and I needed to get requalified. U-2 pilots trained in the T-38 to get more flying time since there were a limited number of U-2s.

We had five checkrides per year, one high flight and low flight in the U-2. We also had a checkride in the mobile car as the backup pilot. In the T-38, we had an instrument and a contract check-ride.

Beale had two of the best T-38 low levels in the country. One skimmed westward across the rice fields to the Pacific Ocean before turning south to end at the Golden Gate Bridge. It provided a stunning view of the San Francisco Bay area. The other low level started at Lake Oroville in Northern California, zigzagging in the canyons up to Lake Tahoe. The track then headed south down to Yosemite National Park where the low level ended. From a pilot's perspective, California offered some of the most incredible views.

In less than a month, I completed T-38 training. I was feeling at home again at Beale and meeting new people every day. Captain Glenn Roberts invited me over for Thanksgiving dinner that year. I met Sherri Juall, my future wife, at his house. We would date over the next ten months before getting married. One of the attendees took a video of that Thanksgiving and later mailed it to us. We labeled it the day we met. I was blessed by everything happening in my life.

My U-2 training partner was Captain Brian Heyne. Brian had a similar story to mine, as he also started out enlisted in the Air Force. We were in Officers School at the same time. After Officers School, Brian got assigned to Laughlin Air Force Base to train as a T-38 instructor.

Our U-2 training started on time but was going to be stretched out. A few months earlier, Saddam Hussein invaded Kuwait, and the squadron sent all available bodies to Taif, Saudi Arabia. We knew the Gulf War would start any day. We were stuck in limbo, as many of us were not fully qualified in the U-2 and could not participate in this war.

In January of 1991, the fireworks started in the Middle East. The initial reports were great, as no U-2 was shot down. That was always a concern in a small squadron since we all knew everybody.

I got a few flights here and there and was able to solo the U-2 in March of that year. Sherri rode in the mobile car and watched me tackle the Dragon Lady alone for the first time.

Once Brian and I soloed, they put us in charge of the Heritage Room. The small room was basically a bar with a keg inside of a refrigerator with various U-2 pictures plastered on the walls. Our job was to make sure the room was clean every morning and never to run out of beer or peanuts.

One early morning, Brian and I had the first launches of the day. We headed home early the night before to get plenty of rest before our flights. Unbeknownst to us, some U-2 pilots decided to have a party in the Heritage Room and left it in a mess. Both Brian and I showed up and flew our flights before checking on the condition of the room. After we landed, we were met by Lt. Col. Rick Bishop, who told us about our responsibilities in keeping the Heritage Room in tip-top shape. From then on, flying was always the second thing to think about when arriving at work. We were relieved when the next group of trainees behind us soloed and took over the job of maintaining the Heritage Room.

Soon the summer months were upon us, as many of us students were backlogged in the training program. Sometimes we had long stretches between our scheduled flights. When that was the case, we would take the boats to the local lake and water ski till we dropped. Then we would set up our tents and camp under the stars. It was a great time for all of us in training. It would be the last summer we were all together. Once we were qualified, the demanding mission requirements would scatter us to all ends of the earth. We all treasured those glorious moments we had that summer.

On my first high-altitude flight, my instructor, Lt. Col. Dan Kelly, and I were scheduled for a two-and-a-half hour sortie. I was ecstatic as I had only flown low flights around the pattern. For the high flight, I had to put on the spacesuit and go where the U-2 was born to go.

The day before, I reviewed all my charts for my route of flight. We would fly over to the coast and then head south to Los Angeles before returning home.

We showed up at PSD early and ate steak and eggs. A cook was assigned to PSD to prepare all the meals for the pilots on high flights. After eating, we headed down to get our physicals. Some of my old friends in PSD were there to greet me. My heartbeat was off the charts, but the PSD guy taking my blood pressure just winked at me and told me to have a good time.

It had been a long time since I was last in the spacesuit. I am sure everyone there could tell I was as nervous. I had heard many stories about the views from flying on the edge of space. Other U-2 pilots had talked about the "Terminator." I was excited to see that, whatever it was.

After thirty minutes of pre-breathing in the suit, Dan and I headed to the jet. I would sit in the front seat now, unlike my interview, where I was in the back seat. All the Dragon Lady controls would be at my disposal.

As I was strapped in, I saw Sherri waving to me. I knew she was as excited as I was. Butterflies swirled around my stomach as I started the engine.

Lining up on the runway, the maintenance crew pulled the pogo pins, and we were ready. I got takeoff clearance and ran the power up to 80% to check my engine instruments one last time. All the gauges were in the green, as I shoved the throttle all the way to the stop. The Dragon Lady roared to life.

I felt like I was holding on for dear life as the plane lifted off shortly and headed skyward at a 35-degree angle. The vertical velocity gauge was pegged. Before I could start breathing, we were passing through 20,000 feet. Wow! This was a rocket ship.

Ten minutes later, we were passing through 52,000 feet. I turned the autopilot on and finally relaxed as the plane continued skyward.

Dan pointed out some of the area landmarks. Lake Tahoe now resembled a small backyard pond as we passed through 60,000 feet.

The sky below was the same blue as when viewed from the ground, but the atmosphere at our altitude and above us was a dark black color. "That is the 'Terminator,'" Dan stated.

As we turned toward the coast, my head kept bumping against the windshield. I was a kid in a candy store, and I had to see everything. The airplane could have been on fire, and I would not have noticed. I was too busy sightseeing.

Some frost started to form on the windshield, but I just brushed it off. The U-2 operated in an unforgiving environment at this altitude. As we started to turn south, I could see the entire coast of California out my left window.

I had previously seen U-2 photos in books, but they did no justice to the view below me. I wanted to stay up here forever.

Eventually, all great things must come to an end. I pulled off some power and threw the gear down. We landed a short time later as a crowd greeted me. I knew I would never forget that first flight. I was also glad the Air Force paid me to fly jets.

After I got checked out in the U-2, Sherri and I got married. We would have to delay our honeymoon as I was scheduled to leave for Korea five days later. We decided to get married on the south shore of Lake Tahoe, an area I had seen many times from the T-38 low levels. We rented a dozen rooms along the beach and played volleyball until someone blew a whistle. That was our signal to get ready for the wedding. Tom Ruggiero and Phil Anderson, my flight school classmates, were my best men. We had the time of our lives. Life couldn't get any better.

South Korea

South Korea was the first stop as a U-2 pilot after training. This was not the first time I had been to Osan AB, South Korea. I had been there ten years earlier when I worked as a PSD technician. I was sure the entire area had changed, and I was excited to see what was new.

The familiar smell of Kimchi overwhelmed my nostrils on the descent into Korea. The scent of Kimchi and other Korean dishes permeates the entire peninsula. It was a different smell than I was used to growing up in America. After a while I got used to it and Korean food would become my favorite.

After arriving in the country, the jet lag and time zone changes leave you in a semi-drunken state. I felt like a zombie as I was introduced to all the other pilots at the Detachment. I was wiped out but had to force myself to stay awake to get on the new schedule. No matter what I did, it usually took me about five days to get through that groggy feeling.

At Detachment 2 we were called the "Black Cats." Everyone in and around the base knew the Black Cats were associated with the U-2, enhancing the mystique. If anybody inquired where you worked, you just said you were a Black Cat. Nobody would ask any more questions. The Black Cats had a pair of U-2s that monitored the DMZ along the Korean peninsula.

The Detachment actually had a black cat they called Oscar. We all were responsible for taking care of and feeding Oscar. There had been many Oscars over the years, as some had met their demise in and around the Detachment. One Oscar had a short life as he was last seen on our electrical transformer outside the building. I am unsure if the lights and communications equipment were knocked out for a while after that incident. It was rumored that one Oscar actually got a flight in the Dragon Lady.

Our dorm rooms were similar to three-story hotel buildings. The U-2 pilots were housed with other pilots, some on temporary duty like us. Some F-15 crews from Kadena AB, Japan, were next to me and rotated out regularly to help supplement the base fighters. All the US and South Korean fighters would provide a daily air cap over South Korea. It sent a powerful signal that we were prepared to defend the country.

Over the next few days, I studied all aspects of flying the Dragon Lady up and down the DMZ. I would be in radio contact the entire flight, the main reason new U-2 pilots went to Korea first.

The first warning on our paperwork is to not fly over the "Blue House." The Blue House, as the Koreans called it, was where their President resided. The Blue House also moved wherever the President moved. It was a challenge to ensure we were not above the Blue House when their President went mobile.

I spent the better part of four days reviewing my mission while still trying to get on the same time zone as everybody else.

On the third night, a couple of other U-2 pilots took me downtown to eat some Bulgogi, a thinly sliced beef dish. The Bulgogi was marinated to perfection. I also ordered some side vegetable dishes. It was fantastic. I had tasted it years earlier but had forgotten how much I loved it. I walked around, glancing to see if any of the old shops and clubs were still around. Many shops had been updated since the 1984 Olympics. Korea's economy took off after the games. The area surrounding the base was not as poor as I remembered it ten years earlier. High-end retailers and manufacturing were everywhere along the main road.

Old Korean women still sold fried dumplings and shrimp near the base gate. Operating with a small cart and a big wok containing hot oil, the women would fry up some goodies in a couple of minutes. The dumplings were always piping hot and would burn the roof of my mouth each time I ate them. I never had the patience to wait for them to cool.

The Detachment had one day off each month. That night we would go downtown and do the Stray Cat Strut by the Stray Cats. Between 50 and 100 Black Cats would line up in a straight line. Each person would put their hands on the shoulders of the person in front of them. Once connected, we would head into the clubs in one big Conga line. As we entered each club, the DJ would play our Stray Cat song, and we would weave back and forth around the tables and then out the door to the next club. The front of the line was often leaving the club as the back of the line was entering. All the spectators knew we were with the Black Cats. This was our song and our night. It was a sight to see.

When pilots landed after operational missions, we all would gather to greet them. It was a tradition we did not have anywhere else in the world, but it made us feel special to have a crowd waiting for us. It was nice to see such camaraderie.

The day before I was scheduled to fly, I was the mobile pilot and the backup pilot. I was responsible for preflighting the cockpit and ensuring the pilot flying had everything they needed. We got up early and ate breakfast, steak and eggs at the chow hall if we could get it. Once done eating, we would head to the squadron to see if anything had changed with mission planning. If everything was a go, the pilot would head to PSD to get dressed. As the backup pilot, I headed out to preflight the Dragon Lady. After I had completed the preflight, I went over to brief the pilot on any last-minute changes. If everything was okay, I would give them a thumbs up.

The mission pilot would pre-breath before heading out to the aircraft. At this time, I just monitored the radios from the chase car and put out any fires that might pop up to prevent an on-time launch.

Once the pilot started the engine and taxied the aircraft, I would follow behind in the car. Out on the runway, I ensured the ground crew pulled the pogo pins and gave the pilot one last thumbs up for takeoff.

After launching the U-2, I returned to the squadron and began planning my mission for the next day.

***

The next day I was beyond nervous as I prepared for my first operational mission in the U-2. A mistake would put me on every nightly news organization worldwide. I took deep breaths to try and calm myself but to no avail. I had the same butterflies in my stomach as I did wrestling in high school.

I jumped in the suit and tried to relax for a bit. The pressure suit did help. I had always felt comfortable in the spacesuit since my PSD days. Breathing 100% pure oxygen tends to cure any stomach or intestinal issues. The calming effect of hearing my breathing through the regulator helped my nerves.

A few minutes later, the mobile pilot came in and gave me a thumbs-up. The Dragon Lady was ready for me. I asked myself, was I ready for the Dragon Lady? Would I be fighting the Dragon or dancing with the Lady on my first mission?

Walking out to the plane was an incredible moment I will never forget. The evaporation from the oxygen bottles from the bottom of the aircraft drifted across the tarmac. Wow, I thought to myself. She looks ominous. The tail of the U-2 had a beautiful painting of a Black Cat. Some maintenance personnel had used red paint to outline the face of a cat with a white mustache. The picture of the cat stood out in contrast to the black paint scheme of the aircraft.

Dozens of antennas protruded out from the bottom of the plane. I had never seen so many antennas on an aircraft. How many electronic boxes were onboard, I wondered. Most pilots never knew how all the electronic equipment inside the wing pods worked. That was where all the magic happened. Since it was not in our training manuals, pilots did not take an interest. Someday, I wanted to find out what this aircraft was really capable of.

Dozens of civilian and military officials surrounded the plane, watching and waiting for the launch. The many civilians were from different organizations from across the US. They supported and ensured their equipment worked as advertised and was always available in case it didn't. The Commander of the Detachment was probably the only person who knew where all the civilians worked.

I sat in the cockpit with my arms stretched outward so PSD could hook me up to the parachute and the seat kit. This part of the job I was familiar with. I smiled at the technicians and thanked them for all their hard work. I knew they lived for an encouraging word every once in a while.

Once I closed the canopy, I called for the engine start. The crew chief signaled for air and cleared me to start. The plane roared to life, as my training began to take over. The nerves subsided somewhat, while my excitement was still through the roof.

Pushing the throttle up, I noticed the plane did not move. Had I forgotten something? I added more power as the Dragon slowly started to creep along. This plane was heavier than any mission I had flown before. I never had a training mission flying with a full load of fuel. The Dragon Lady could hold twenty thousand pounds of fuel, half the aircraft's weight. Finally, the aircraft was taxiing at a comfortable speed.

I got clearance from the tower and lined up on runway 27 for a westerly takeoff. After the ground crew retrieved my pogo pins, I glanced over and got a thumbs-up from the mobile pilot.

Confirming my instruments all looked good, I took a deep breath and shoved the throttle to the limit. The Dragon Lady roared to life and started down the runway. It was slower than I anticipated due to the aircraft's weight.

The Dragon Lady lifted off at 1700 feet down the runway and began her ascent. The clock had started on my nine-hour mission today, the standard mission for Korea. The climb angle was still great even at this maximum weight. At 52,000 feet, I turned on the autopilot and all the electronic equipment. I sat back as the autopilot took control of the plane and entered the orbit track.

Each racetrack around the Korean peninsula took about an hour. The autopilot would turn the plane 180 degrees when it hit the Yellow Sea and then repeat when it reached the Sea of Japan. This worked out to eight orbit patterns with the extra hour for climbing and descending.

For the first hour, I kept bumping my head against the canopy, a bad habit I picked up on my first high flight in training. I couldn't stop looking outside at all the new sights. I was excited to see what North Korea looked like, but it resembled the rest of the continent. There were no visible cities in the north, and Pyongyang was too far away to see with the naked eye. Seoul was the exception in the South. Seoul was large and sprawled out over many miles. With 10.5 million people taking up residence in the city, it resembled Los Angeles.

I marked my orbit times on my flight boards as I passed over each navigational point. This ensured I stayed on track for each orbit.

The camera and electronic gear were controlled by the ground personnel. I paid little attention to them as I could not see or hear anything they were looking at. The intelligence people on the ground had all the good information as we pilots just got to see the beautiful sights.

Nearing my fourth hour, I decided to write to my wife and tell her about my first mission. I pulled out my pen and paper and started putting together a letter. It wasn't too long before I felt a slight pain in my fingers. I knew it was the nitrogen bubbles collecting in my joints. The pre-breathing we did an hour before our flight did not remove all of the nitrogen in our bloodstream. What little nitrogen was left would congregate around the joints. This symptom was called the bends and could be painful. I knew better since I had taught the bends while working in PSD. I shook my head, thinking how stupid I could be, I should have known better. It was the last letter I ever wrote while flying in the Dragon Lady.

It was time to eat. I was too scared to try the bacon and eggs, so I stuck to the applesauce and pears. It was better than nothing, but not enough to fill my stomach, probably for the better, as I was unsure how my body would react on such a long flight. The process of eating takes place in miles. I tried to make it last a hundred miles before starting on my drinks. I decided to go with the trusted orange juice and water on my first flight. All my drinks stayed cold as the cockpit was chilly, with frost on the windshield. The suit kept me at a comfortable seventy degrees as I could control the amount of air through the vent. If I wanted cooler air, I turned up the vent. If I wanted warmer air, I shut off the vent and my body temperature would warm me up.

On my sixth orbit, the excitement of flying my first operation mission started to wear off. This flight was now the longest flight I had ever flown in the U-2. I had seen all the sights multiple times and couldn't wait to get down. The thrill of being a U-2 pilot was starting to wear off.

The last hour was the hardest as I started talking to myself. It had been a long day. I kept thinking about the descent and couldn't wait to head back down to earth. I had not prepared myself for such a long mission, although how do you prepare for something like that?

The mobile pilot radioed to see how I was doing. It was nice to hear a voice over the radio instead of my breathing. I didn't want to tell them I was dying of boredom as they might think I was a wimpy pilot.

Finally, the descent point arrived and I started the checklist to head down. As I put the gear down and the speed brakes out, the aircraft slowly started its descent. I was excited that my first flight was uneventful and that I had not screwed up.

Lining up on the runway, I wondered how landing an operational U-2 might compare to landing a training aircraft. I glanced down and noticed I had burned almost all of the fuel I had started with. I said a quick prayer as I saw the mobile car lined up beside the runway.

Crossing the runway threshold, the mobile started making his calls. I tried to hold the plane off at two feet and let her tail slowly come down. The heavy aircraft was more stable than the lighter U-2s I had flown in training. My landing was uneventful, and I breathed a sigh of relief. I had completed my first operational mission. I was proud of not damaging the Dragon Lady or killing myself.

Once I got the plane shut down, I opened the canopy and was amazed to see several dozen people there to greet me. Maybe they thought I would crash the plane and wanted to see the show. I was glad to disappoint them.

Coming down the aircraft stairs, I felt the effects of a long day at the office. A temporary Assistant Director of Operations (ADO) asked me how the flight was. I chuckled and said I never wanted to do that again. I was joking, of course, but he was mad at me and thought that was disrespectful to say. At this point in my day, I could have cared less. I was exhausted and wanted to eat dinner and head to bed.

***

A couple of weeks later, I was the mobile for Captain Rich Schneider. Rich was a great guy and had been to Korea several times. I respected him and his knowledge of the aircraft.

Osan was having one of their monthly exercises that lasted for days and into the nights. Loud booms and sirens echoed all over the base, simulating an attack. Sleeping at night in the dorms was next to impossible.

Since we were flying operational missions, we were exempt from the drills and did not have to wear chemical gear like the rest of the troops. We possessed a letter of exemption and had to present it at every checkpoint to get to work.

During these drills, we were authorized to sleep in the deep underground part of the hospital that was shielded from all the noise.

Several of the crews before us had opted to sleep there, but Rich decided his own bed would be best. That was fine with me. I was going to follow him wherever he went. I was his wingman, or backup pilot, in this case. If he wanted to sleep outside in a tent, I would be right beside him. I was not going to leave him.

The next day, after I launched Rich, that same temporary ADO started yelling at me because Rich and I did not sleep at the hospital. I told him I was going wherever Rich went since I was his backup. He continued to berate me as it got a little heated. I thought it odd he would come after me instead of waiting until Rich landed and confronting him. After all, it was Rich's decision, not mine.

When Rich landed, nobody said anything to him. I guess it was me the ADO was after. Years later, he would finally apologize to me. He told me he was mad at me for my comments after my first flight. I was surprised he remembered my comment and carried that hatred for so many years. Soon afterward, Major Mario Buda was back as Operations Officer and life was back to normal.

***

About halfway through flying a night mission, I got a call over the data link. The voice asked me if I had seen an explosion off my right wing in the direction of North Korea.

With my interest piqued, I scanned almost the entire country of the Communist regime. Nothing was visible, not even a light bulb. I knew North Korea had electricity, but everything was pitch black, unlike Seoul, which was lit up like a Christmas tree and could be seen from space.

I took a deep breath and informed the individual that I could see no visible signs of an explosion. The intelligence guy nonchalantly said thanks and didn't say another word. Now curiosity was killing me. I asked them what they thought it was. He informed me that all their earthquake counters recorded a large explosion north of my position. Now, this had my attention on an otherwise boring flight.

I continued glancing around the aircraft and even looked through the little periscope to spot anything directly below the aircraft. Flying above 70,000 feet, we could not look over the side and see straight down, but the periscope enabled us to accomplish that.

Nothing. I could not see a fireball or anything in the black of the night. I started thinking about a Plan B if things started to go south. Where would I head to? I thought Kadena Air Base, on the island of Okinawa, was a good option. That would be away from any of the fighting. The crazy thing was that if a war did kick off, all the planes from Kadena would be heading in my direction. My boss might not be too impressed if I bugged out early and fled the fighting.

I landed late that night and went to bed without much thought about what had transpired. The following day I turned on CNN and saw a story about an explosion at an Army barracks in North Korea. There was not much to the story, and I thought it must have been an accident.

Later that day, I went to the intelligence center, and they showed me a photograph my plane had taken during my mission. The photo showed an enormous crater at a military site. They had pre- and post-pictures of the exact same location. The crater was nearly 700 feet wide, with debris scattered out to 1500 feet from the epicenter. Several Army barracks were wiped off the face of the planet. I wondered if there were any North Korean troops sleeping in those barracks. If there were, they were dead now. This was the only time I ever saw an actual photograph that my plane had taken. I was astonished at the clarity; it brought new meaning to the capabilities of the Dragon Lady.

***

Winter was approaching as I flew my last mission for this tour. As I entered the orbit, the first loop was choppy. On the second orbit, the turbulence got even worse. I was encountering a pretty good ride in the Dragon, causing the plane to start oscillating in the pitch mode. The DMZ held a dark little secret during the winter months. The unstable atmosphere at 70,000 feet could bite you quickly if you were not prepared to take action.

The U-2 offered little room between a stall and an overspeed. In one moment, you could exceed your cruise speed and the next be out of airspeed. It was a nerve-wracking ride on the edge of the U-2's capabilities.

Eventually, my autopilots shut off, causing me to hand fly the aircraft. On normal occasions, that is not a big deal, but we needed the autopilot to fly above 52,000 feet. I eased the airplane into a gradual turn to head back in the opposite direction with smoother air. I knew I had to get out of the turbulence before I lost control of the plane. I had never experienced this kind of roughness at altitude in my limited U-2 experience.

I knew going off track this close to Seoul I didn't want to overfly the Blue House or accidentally fly into North Korea. My heart was pounding as I struggled to get the Dragon Lady back on track and out of the turbulence. Once established in my orbit, I called Ops and told them I was cutting my orbit short. My mobile confirmed my new plan of only flying the western part of the orbit.

On the next orbit, the turbulence kicked off my autopilot just after I started to head east. The turbulence was now affecting the entire orbit, and I was struggling to fly the aircraft by hand. My only choice now was to descend to give me more room between the stall and the overspeed margins.

I descended 5,000 feet as the turbulence seemed to follow me down in altitude. It was a no-win situation. When the autopilot did stay connected, it was a roller coaster ride up and down. I was frustrated that my briefing guide did not mention anything about this kind of turbulence in Korea.

Finally, my time was up and I started my descent. I was completely exhausted, both mentally and physically, from flying the aircraft. It was the roughest flight I would ever have in the U-2 for the rest of my career.

Two months later, we would lose Captain Marty McGregor to that same turbulence in Korea. Nowhere in the world did we ever encounter turbulence like we did in Korea.

The funerals were the hardest part of the job. Marty's funeral was tough as they had a couple of kids. It was hard to hold back all our emotions. We could only think about the good times we had with Marty during training. My wife and I did not say much. We had only been married for five months. I know she was wondering if I might not come home someday. But being a pilot was no different than being a police officer or a firefighter. Some day the Dragon may get me too.

***

On another tour, I was the mobile for Major Chauncey Gardner. He was scheduled for a late afternoon launch and would land around midnight. The launch was uneventful, but a few hours later the heat from the day fueled some massive Cumulonimbus clouds. These rapid building storms were commonplace in Korea during the summer months.

By nine o'clock at night, all hell had broken loose. The lightning show was in full force. The center of the tremendous storm lay just west of Osan but was closing in on our location. Chauncey was scheduled to land in three hours, and I knew I would have my hands full, so I called in another U-2 pilot to help me out.

We headed to base operations to talk to the weather guy to see if there were any holes in the storm we might be able to get Chauncey through. We were surprised to hear that the weatherman had gone home to bed. At first, I thought there must be some mistake, as we had an airborne aircraft. We told the admin guy to call the weatherman up and get him back to work.

We patrolled around the runway with some time to pass, waiting for the weatherman to show up. No other aircraft were flying as the base was pretty much shut down. The storm was getting louder and meaner as eleven o'clock approached.

Finally, a dreary-eyed weatherman showed up to base operations. We asked him to take a look at the weather radar to see what our options were. He immediately informed us he could not turn the radar on since the storm may damage it. At this point, I lost it. My tone did not gradually rise; it started near the top of my vocal range. I screamed at him that we had a pilot up there and we needed to get him down.

The weatherman held his own, saying he was only following orders. I got on the phone, and we started going up the chain of command to the base commander. We needed to get authorization to turn the base radar back on.

What would I tell Chauncey's wife and kids if something happened? The base would not let me turn on their radar for fear it may be damaged by the storm.

By this time, Chauncey had already descended to 40,000 and was awaiting our direction since he had no radar on the U-2. The storm grew even more intense and now was one of the nastiest storms I had ever seen. Growing up in Kansas, I had seen some big storms, but this one matched anything I could remember.

We did our best to stay in communication with Chauncey, but the lightning and electrical interference made talking with him a challenge. At one point, he said he may have to eject because he was having a hard time controlling the Dragon. How did we get this far down the road, I thought to myself. None of this was in our weather briefing before the launch.

We thought about diverting him to another base, but the storm was overhanging the entire country of South Korea. Our only other option was to keep him airborne until the storm passed over Osan.

We gave Chauncey the okay to come in from the west an hour later. The winds were swirling all around and we thought it best if Chauncey circled to land on runway 27. When he was approaching the runway, it was pitch black and I struggled to even see the plane while giving altitude calls. The mobile car was sliding back and forth while I was chasing the U-2 down the runway.

Finally, Chauncey got the Dragon Lady stopped. I pulled the car around in front of the aircraft and was astonished at what I saw. Parts of the nose cone on the aircraft were dangling free, barely held on by the remaining fiberglass. Both of the engine inlets were ripped apart, exposing the insides of the engine bay. Did all the missing pieces go through the engine itself, I wondered? The amount of hail damage on the plane nearly brought her down. The Dragon had reared its ugly head on this flight. We were lucky that night that nobody died.

Our amazing maintenance crew would have that plane up and flying again in record time.

***

The Jin-wi River snakes around runway 27 at Osan Air Base in South Korea like a serpent coming out of the sea. It highlighted the mysticism of the Korean peninsula. The sun was setting, and I was approaching the end of my nine-hour mission flying over the DMZ.

I knew the cool air would make the Jin-wi River come alive and bring the fog rolling toward the runway only a few hundred yards away. All my options started filtering through my head. Would I make it down before the fog rolled in, or would I have to divert to Kunsan? Kunsan Air Base was an additional half-hour south of Osan and would extend my duty day even longer. As I started the descent in the U-2, I glanced down and saw the fog on the move. Yikes, I thought to myself, this is going to be close.

Ahead of me was a C-130 gunship getting ready to start the approach to runway 27 at Osan.

I was glad to let him be the guinea pig and see if he could break out of the weather. No luck; a few minutes later, the C-130 called missed approach and advised the tower they were heading to their alternate. The tower controller asked the C-130 what he thought the visibility was, and the C-130 Captain replied, "An eighth of a mile."

After hearing the visibility was 1/8 of a mile, I knew I could not legally start the approach under Air Force rules. I needed at least 1/4 mile visibility. About that time, I heard my commander come on the radio and say, "Why don't you go ahead and try the approach."

Now, I knew I was in a pickle. If I shot the approach and cracked up this multi-million dollar aircraft, I would be in trouble for starting the approach below legal minimums. After a few seconds, I asked my commander over the radio, "Do you want me to start the approach with only 1/8 of a mile visibility?" Now, I put the ball back in his court. I needed a "get out of jail free card" if something happened.

After a few more seconds, my commander replied, "Just go ahead and proceed to Kunsan."

In less than an hour I was circling over Kunsan, but the controller would not give me landing clearance. It was close to midnight on a Friday night, and I was exhausted after flying 10 hours by myself. My patience was wearing thin. I could see another fog bank over the Yellow Sea in the distance, closing in on Kunsan. Oh boy, please let me land, I thought. I wanted to avoid diverting to my second alternate, Okinawa, Japan. That would be another hour and a half of flying time.

Finally, the controller gave me clearance to land. Later I found out the Ops Group Commander was trying to recruit some pilots out of the Officer's Club to help me after I landed. I guess the Officer's Club didn't close until midnight. That was the reason the controller would not let me land.

After I landed in Kunsan, I thought the most challenging part was over, but it was not. The Ops Group Commander had decided he wanted the U-2 in a hangar on the other side of the airfield. Since my pogo wheels were in Osan, I needed help keeping my wings off of the runway. For the next hour, I taxied at a walking pace while I had three half-inebriated fighter pilots holding up each wing, with three additional pilots lying on the top of the wing. I am not sure they realized I didn't need people lying on top of the wing, but I didn't have the heart to tell them otherwise. They were doing their best to get me out of a jam.

At one point, we encountered a steel arresting cable across the taxiway. This taxiway was used as an alternate runway in case the main runway was destroyed during a war. I was informed the cable could not be disconnected and that I would have to taxi over it. I knew this would be a problem in the U-2 since my tailwheel was made of hard plastic, unlike a regular inflated tire. After pushing and swaying from a dozen crewmembers on the tail, the U-2 made it over the arresting cable, but I lost all my ability to steer the aircraft. From now on, I had to have help pushing my tail left and right to move the plane from side to side. Eventually, we made it into one of the hangars.

After finally getting out of my spacesuit, I realized I had no clothes. Lo and behold, that same Ops Group Commander gave me his flight suit and a pair of boots to change into. So for one day, this ole Major got to walk around as a full bird Colonel at Kunsan AB.

The next day around noon, the Calvary from Osan arrived and fixed my tail wheel, as another pilot flew it back home to Osan. I followed behind in the mobile car. My divert was one of the longest flights I had ever flown in the U-2.

I would always be grateful to the wonderful people of Kunsan for taking care of me and my Dragon Lady on Friday night a long time ago.

Saudi Arabia

To get to Saudi Arabia, we had to ride in the back of a KC-135 tanker. Another U-2 pilot, Captain Kevin Henry, would join me on the sixty-day tour to the sandbox. Kevin was going as the Director of Operations. I would be the lowly slug that would get to fly all the operational missions, which was fine by me. Not being in charge of anything in the military has its benefits.

For the first leg, we flew to RAF Mildenhall in England. We sat for a few days before continuing to Taif, Saudi Arabia. It was a nice pit stop to land in Mildenhall, as it would be our last time to have a sip of beer and enjoy the luxuries of Western civilization. We treasured every moment in England, but two days were not nearly enough to get down to London and see the sights.

Jumping back on the same aircraft, we headed to Taif. The flight was about seven hours. We were a little apprehensive about what the desert would hold for us. This would be the first time I had ever been in the Middle East. Little did I know at the time, it would not be my last.

Touching down in the morning hours, we clamored out of the aircraft to be met by a few Air Force officials and some Saudi customs people.

As we gathered off to the side of the tanker, I noticed an American-made F-5 coming down the main runway too fast. The plane crashed into a building a few hundred yards from us. There was no fireball, only a large cloud of dust. I looked at Kevin and asked, "Did you see that?"

He nodded, and it took a moment for us to process what we just saw. A crash had happened right in front of us. I knew instantly the pilot did not survive, as there was no parachute floating from the sky.

Immediately, the local Saudi officials began to escort us into a building as the fire trucks started to show up at the crash site. The Saudis did not want us on the ramp watching the rescue for some reason. It didn't matter, as we had just seen it and could not erase it from our memory. It was another reminder of the dangers of flying high-speed military jets. Sometimes the consequences can be devastating.

Once we processed in, I met my Commander, Lt. Col. Tom Danielson. Tom was on a one-year rotation in Taif. He flew the SR-71 until the Air Force retired it and then switched over to fly the U-2. He was halfway through his tour, and you could tell he was ready to return to the States. I was glad I was only here for sixty days. We all then proceeded to the squadron, where we met a few personnel and quickly finished processing in.

Taif had many other aircraft squadrons during the Gulf War, but now the U-2 squadron was the only one remaining. The only other Americans at Taif were a few contractors.

We soon headed out to the complex we would call home for our time at Taif. The highways were in terrific shape for a country in the desert. The Germans had built the Saudi road system, and you could tell.

Nearly every Saudi drove a Mercedes Benz. In the States, we treated the Mercedes as a luxury car. The Saudis treated the Mercedes as an all-terrain vehicle. It was common to see Saudis off-road in the desert assembling a tent to camp out for the night. These were not your typical American camping tents. These were relatively large with beautiful Persian rugs laid out on the sand. Some even had TV sets and generators for the power source.

Another difference in our cultures was at stoplights. When the light turned green, all the cars behind you would start to honk their horns. This is to let you know the light had turned green, and it was time for you to go. We would have considered this rude in the States, but it was regarded as a friendly reminder in the Kingdom.

Every once in a while a caravan of Bedouins and their camels appeared out of the desert to cross a highway. They would soon disappear in the sand dunes as quickly as they had appeared. The Bedouins carried with them all their life possessions and essentials needed to survive the harsh environment. Saudi Arabia had a modern culture and a Biblical culture clashing together in the same space.

Our housing complex was large and came with an Olympic size swimming pool and a gymnasium. A few of us military personnel were mixed in with McDonnell Douglas civilian contractors who supported the Saudi F-15s. High concrete walls lined the complex, with one lone guard at the front gate to protect the entire facility.

Taif was on the edge of the "escarpment," as everyone called it. The town sat at an elevation slightly above 6,100 feet. The days were pleasant, and the nights were cool. The landscape was a mixture of mostly rocks with some sand and resembled life on the moon. At least Taif did not have the giant sand dunes with nothing else to see.

On my second day, we took a break and headed to the escarpment's edge. You could look down the valley nearly sixty miles to Mecca. The drop-off was about 2,000 feet straight down. Monkeys played daredevil games with each other along the cliffs. They would harass the visitors for any morsels of food they could get or steal if an opportunity presented itself. It was truly breathtaking to see. I did not expect to see something like this in Saudi Arabia.

Taif also had the local "chop chop" square. The square was where the local officials executed the sentencing for crimes committed. If you were a thief, you probably would lose a hand. Sometimes there were large crowds to watch these events, primarily men. The Saudis would make sure the Westerners were funneled up to the front to witness their type of punishment. Crime was almost non-existent in the Kingdom, and these events reminded everyone why.

On another night we decided to go downtown to the local gold market. It consisted of a dozen nice square tents in a circular pattern around a large fountain. All the tents had red carpets and red backgrounds to show off their shiny gold trinkets. It was breathtaking to see so much gold. Some gold was molded into lengths that extended from head to toe. Some gold outfits weighed almost a full pound or more. All the retailers barely made any profit as the gold was sold near market price. It was a heck of a deal. I stocked up on some rings and necklaces for my wife. I knew the hardship my wife was going through would be dampened if I came home with some treasures.

There were no security guards to be found around the gold market. Since you could lose a hand as a thief, no one in their right mind was going to steal anything.

I was on the schedule for my first mission five days after arriving. It was enough time to get over the jet lag, which was not too bad since I had a few days in England to adjust for some of those hours.

The day before my flight, I was the mobile for Captain Troy Devine. I was happy to see Troy since I had not seen her since my wedding day. This was her last mission in Saudi Arabia. Troy was scheduled to take the same KC-135 aircraft back to California that I had come over on.

The Kingdom of Saudi Arabia did not have female pilots. They did not even want Troy to talk on the radio. On Troy's first mission, she had to radio back her positions to operations and then they would relay that to the tower and approach control. It was awkward, but we followed their customs for her first flight. We all realized how dangerous this was and finally convinced the Saudis to let her talk on the radio like everybody else.

Many people credited Martha McSally as the first woman in the US to fly combat missions in 1995. Troy was logging O1 combat time over Iraq in December of 1991. Troy would never say anything, even as she testified later in Congress about women flying in combat. Troy herself even acknowledges that some female KC-135 tanker pilots were "in the box" and over Iraq refueling the F-117 during Desert Storm. The sad part was those female tanker pilots would never get the recognition they deserved.

Troy would eventually take over as the Commander of the 99RS at Beale. She would retire a few years after that as a Colonel.

Before I left for Taif, my wife and I were looking for a new home. We searched extensively but had had no luck as I headed out the door. I told her if she found anything she liked, buy it. A few days after I arrived in Taif, she called. She had the perfect home in a great neighborhood but needed my signature on all the documents. At the time we did not have the internet, so she faxed all the documents to Taif for me to sign. We set up two fax machines, one to receive the fax and one to transmit it back to my wife. In those days the fax paper was one continuous sheet. As soon as the fax came out, I signed where an X was and fed the paper into the second machine. I didn't have time to read any of the pages and assumed my wife had done that. Ten minutes later, the whole process was completed and we had a new house. It was the easiest house I would ever buy.

The missions over Iraq were different from the racetrack patterns I experienced in Korea. The Iraqi missions consisted of flying over Iraq to different spots and then returning to Taif. Each mission had a different track as we relieved our targets from the United Nations. It sounded pretty straightforward.

Unlike Korea, I would not talk to anybody except for Taif Tower. This mission would consist of eight hours of talking to myself, which I was getting used to.

Waking up in the mornings was not a problem. You did not need an alarm clock in Saudi Arabia, as the prayers over the loudspeakers started before sunrise.

The morning of my flight, my mission planner woke up before prayer time and made me breakfast. Making me breakfast was not in his job description, so I really appreciated his effort. Since the compound dining facility did not open until 9 am, we had to improvise on breakfast. There would be no steak and eggs like we had in Korea and the US.

Meals Ready to Eat (MREs) were on the breakfast menu for today. Our squadron had pallets of MREs left over from the Gulf War. Cases of them were stacked up against the wall at our house. My mission planner did his best job with what he had to work with. He would scavenge through five or six MREs to find the best items to make breakfast. The problem was, most of the MREs contained lunch items. Spaghetti, beef stroganoff, and mac and cheese were my favorites. I was not used to eating these items for breakfast but promised myself not to complain. We both made the best of our situation. On a good note, the MREs were better than the tube food I had to eat in the Dragon Lady.

As I headed airborne to the unknown, there was nothing but sand dunes upon sand dunes for as far as the eye could see. There was not much to see while looking out the window. Korea had mountains and forests, whereas Saudi Arabia was all sand, or so I thought.

About an hour after takeoff, I noticed green circles in the middle of the desert ahead of me. I checked my map boards only to find the town of Hail, Saudi Arabia listed on the map. I was intrigued. Was this an oasis in the middle of the desert, or just a mirage? Maybe I was seeing things.

Ten minutes later, I was over the small town of Hail, and circle irrigation crops were everywhere. To my amazement, these were the green-colored circles I had seen 70 miles back. It indeed was an oasis. There were no reservoirs or rivers in sight to bring water to the area. I figured the water had to be from underground irrigation wells. I was not expecting to see such a lush area in the middle of nowhere.

Thirty minutes later, I was crossing into Iraq. It had been an hour since I had last talked to a soul. I did not mind the peace and quiet. The Dragon Lady turned to the right, heading for its first target. I could feel the slight vibration of the radar camera moving up front in the nose cone. The target list had little rhyme or reason for me as a pilot. It didn't matter, as the camera could film a swath a few hundred miles wide.

I was not worried about any enemy aircraft as none had taken any actions against the U-2s so far. The United Nations also limited the Iraqis from flying jets above the 36th parallel and below the 32nd parallel. I assumed this limitation on Saddam Hussein, a Sunni, was to prevent him from attacking the Shiites in the south or the Kurds in the northern part of Iraq.

As I closed in on Baghdad, there was no radio chatter to speak of. It was an eerie feeling being so quiet. A hundred miles back I flew over a couple of military airfields and saw no movement of any aircraft. This was unusual, I told myself.

Over Baghdad, I found myself bumping my head on the canopy again. How stupid I was, I thought. If I scratched up my helmet, PSD would be furious at me. I could see the Euphrates and Tigris rivers to my left. Both rivers met in Bagdad. This was supposedly the Garden of Eden, as I recalled from my Sunday school classes. Close to the rivers, I could see green crops here and there, but I saw the area vertically instead of on the ground.

I looked through the periscope, zooming in on downtown Baghdad. I spotted some of the larger palaces, but I had no idea what their names were. It didn't matter; the camera and Intel personnel would figure it out. Was Saddam down there in one of those palaces? Who knew? I sure didn't.

The aircraft turned north to follow the Tigris River up to Tikrit, Saddam's hometown. My last point was to cross over Mosul, the furthest north I would go today. It was apparent that civilization in Iraq was closely intertwined with the Tigris and Euphrates Rivers, winding throughout the country. It only made sense for survival reasons.

On my return leg, I paralleled the Syrian border as the Dragon Lady scanned the western part of Iraq and its few military bases. This was a long flight over inhospitable terrain. It would be challenging if something happened and I had to eject. I was not overly confident the locals would be too receptive to see me. The locals usually take the brunt of any conflict, and I would be an easy target for revenge.

Crossing back into Saudi Arabia, I breathed a little easier as I prepared for my descent into Taif. Overall, I was happy there was not much going on over Iraq. Boring was better than dodging air intercepts from MiG 25s. The Iraqis still had a few operational military fighter jets that avoided the US bombings.

As I contacted Taif approach control, they told me to turn off my cameras as I passed over Mecca. I chuckled to myself as I had already turned the cameras off leaving Iraq. I reassured the controllers the camera was not on.

I set up for an uneventful landing and was glad to have completed my first mission. As I taxied in, the area was busy as a beehive. Civilian contractors were present to offload the film and immediately load it onto a waiting transport aircraft heading to the United States. Within an hour of landing, the film I had taken from my mission was airborne.

My debrief was short and sweet, and I inquired when our next flight might be. I was told by my Commander we didn't have another mission scheduled for ten days. Ten days, I thought. That was a long time in-between missions to find something to do.

That February, we flew three missions over Iraq, and I flew all of them. I then proceeded to fly three out of the four missions the next month before returning home. I was not sure why the United Nations didn't want us to fly more missions. That was way above my pay grade, and it was not my place to question their directives.

Those two months were boring with not much to do. There are only so many times a person can venture out in the desert trying to find entertainment to pass the time.

***

A little more than a year later, I returned to Taif for another two months. I had hoped it would be better than the last time I was here.

It was. We now stayed in some single-wide trailers right across from the base. The trailers were a step up since they saved us a lot of time traveling between work and home. Somehow, the squadron obtained about twenty-five trailers and set up a nice little community. We had a small gathering place, a library, and an above-ground swimming pool. Several nights a week, we would crank up the barbeque and cook up some hamburgers and hot dogs. We reminisced about life in the States around the BBQ pit. This housing setup felt like we were all family instead of being so spread out in the other compound.

Since Taif's temperature was near freezing most nights, the pool was not used. Even with the daytime temperatures in the 90s, it was not enough to heat the water to a desired comfort level. We set out immediately to resolve the cool temperature issue for our pool. We requested a water pump from our supply personnel and headed to the military dump. The dump was a maze of military and housing parts thrown all together in a heap after the war. We found six mini water heaters and headed back to the trailers. The Saudis paid for our electricity, so we powered up all the water heaters and connected them inline. The pump ran cold water in, and the heaters dispensed warmer water back into the little pool. It worked. A few days later, the temperature in the swimming pool was a comfortable 80 degrees. We could now swim during the day and even on some of the cooler nights. Along with the BBQ and the pool, life was pretty good.

The squadron also had a new chow hall since I was there last. The Saudis provided Sri Lankan cooks for us. They could make a feast out of a small budget. One time, we asked if they could prepare smoked salmon for Thanksgiving. They gave us a puzzled look but nodded in agreement. On Thanksgiving Day we showed up with anticipation for some smoked salmon. To our surprise, they had smoked salmon. They prepared a large salmon and shoved a pack of cigarettes inside the salmon's mouth. We laughed with hysteria as the Sri Lankans tried to understand what was so funny. Somebody finally spilled the beans, and they started laughing along with us. The cultural differences were too much for smoked salmon. We did have the best cooks in the Kingdom, and we knew it. We treated them like royalty and were grateful for all their creations. They all worked for minimum pay and just wanted to please us. They were such good cooks; soon a visiting general took them from us and moved them to Riyadh.

Our Squadron Commander, Lt. Colonel Chuck Wilson, requested and got approval for some day passes in Jeddah at a resort on the beach. A day at the beach was better than roaming around the desert looking for Bedouins.

Jeddah was a modern city compared to Taif. Jeddah had roundabouts throughout the city with unusual artwork in the center of them. One had old cars sticking out of a large concrete square block. Another roundabout had a car flying on top of a rug. We didn't understand the deeper meaning but applauded the Saudi efforts to spruce up the desert. Modern shopping centers were located across the city and resembled life back home. I went in and bought some perfume for my wife. Any time we got off, we spent at the resort in Jeddah. Snorkeling in the Red Sea was spectacular. The water was crystal clear and vibrant with life. I was not in Kansas anymore.

Beale AFB had sent my boss Chuck over without even being qualified in the U-2. He had some of his training in the States, but time ran out and they needed him in Taif. Since I was a check pilot, the commanders in the States thought I could give Chuck a checkride and finish him up in Taif. This was highly unusual as we never gave checkrides at our temporary deployments. So we gave Chuck a practice ride and then a checkride on his next flight. He passed with flying colors. Most old-time U-2 pilots flew the Dragon Lady better than the young guns. The old guys knew every sneaky trick the ole Dragon Lady had up her sleeve.

***

I felt relaxed before my first mission since I had flown six flights the last time I was in Taif. The Iraqis were much more active now than the previous year. I put in more effort into studying the capabilities of the Iraqi MiG 25 and MiG 29 aircraft. Iraq was flying over 300 military missions on some days, while we were still flying alone with no fighter cap support. Granted, many Iraqi military flights were helicopters, but they also were launching a fair amount of fighter jets.

Before coming to Saudi for this trip, I had to get a United Nations passport. We would carry the UN passport on all flights and leave any US identification or markings at the squadron. The Dragon Lady even had the letters UN painted on its tail and underneath the wings. I was not sure it would stop the Iraqis from trying to shoot me down, though. If it were up to me, I would have painted "Don't shoot" on the bottom of each wing.

I blasted off again early in the morning. The town of Hail, Saudi Arabia, still looked the same. The green irrigation circles stuck out in contrast to the sand-colored landscape.

Closing in on the Iraqi border, I contacted the Airborne Warning and Control System (AWACS) and checked in. AWACS was like an airborne tower that controlled all the airspace they could see with their radar. Communicating with AWACS was something new as tensions were on a higher level now. I was happy to have another US aircraft to help monitor the skies for me. For years, U-2 pilots prided themselves on not talking to anybody for the entire flight. Silence was a risky bet in today's modern warfare.

Everything was normal until I flew above the 32nd parallel. AWACS informed me that a MiG 25 Foxbat was on an intercept course for me and was 150 miles in front of me. I had never been intercepted before and was calculating in my head the best course of action if they got closer. There would be no sightseeing on this flight as I could feel my heart pumping beneath my spacesuit. The Dragon Lady was not a nimble aircraft, and I could not yank and bank at this altitude to avoid a missile. If I did that, the wings would fall off. With no fighter cap for protection, my only option was to turn away and run.

AWACS continued calling out the Iraqi fighters' distance from me. I knew there had to be some time lag when AWACS radioed me the information. I calculated when the MiG hit 60 miles; I would break off my flight plan and turn to the left, away from Baghdad. I knew the Foxbat could only fly straight and level wings nearing my altitude. If he had to adjust his angle to match my turn, his plane would go out of control. When AWACS called 70 miles, I put my hand on the autopilot turn knob. I did not want to turn the autopilot off and have to think about flying the plane with a MiG on my tail. By using the turn knob, the autopilot would still control the aircraft while I could keep my thoughts on the MiG. Things had changed quite a bit since my flights the year before. Why did we have to go through this on approved UN flights? The Dragon wasn't raising its ugly head; Saddam was.

Just then a voice yelled over the radio, "He's breaking it off."

I breathed a sigh of relief as I took my hand off the turn knob and let the plane continue on its course. A Rivet Joint (RJ) KC-135 aircraft came over the radio again and informed me the Iraqi pilot was ending the engagement due to equipment malfunctions on his aircraft.

While AWACS provided me with the enemy's whereabouts, RJ could give me the enemy's intentions with their electronic and linguist specialists onboard. Together, both aircraft gave me a complete picture of everything going on in my airspace.

I didn't care why the Iraqi pilot decided to end his intercept, but I was sure an aircraft equipment malfunction was not the culprit. He probably knew there would be repercussions for launching a missile at me—if he even had a missile. In times like this, I wished I had a few missiles myself.

The rest of the flight was uneventful, but my nerves were shot for the remainder of the day. During the debrief, I explained everything that happened. The same intercepts were happening to the other pilots as well. We were all upset about the situation. I could tell my Commander Chuck Wilson was unhappy and knew something needed to change.

***

On another mission, I was running late to get suited up. I was heading to the bathroom one last time when the mission planner forgot to brief me on some late intelligence. Once briefed, I rushed over to PSD and suited up. During my pre-breathing time, I remembered that I had forgotten to go to the bathroom. No big deal I thought, I would go in the plane after I got airborne.

Climbing out of Taif, everything went normally. It was a beautiful October day in the Kingdom, just like the day before and just like the next day would be. A weatherman in Saudi Arabia had the dream job.

I clicked on the autopilot and started to dial in some pressure on the primary controller on my suit. To go to the bathroom, I didn't need much pressure, just enough to ensure the airflow in the suit forced urine through my UCD. Once the suit was partially inflated, I started to go number one. It's not easy for a guy to go to the bathroom sitting down. Today was not the case, as I had a full bladder and could not wait any longer.

I immediately noticed that something was wrong. I could feel a warm feeling around my leg. Oh no, I thought. My UCD was kinked and was not letting the urine flow through the tube. I tried to stop, but it was too late. I cussed myself out for not going to the bathroom before takeoff. A few minutes later, I was finished. I had urine all underneath my buttocks area. To make matters worse, my left boot was half full, too. I hadn't even reached the town of Hail yet, but I was about to go through it.

Looking down at the clock, I realized that I had eight and a half hours left on this mission. I almost started to cry. What should I do now? I could declare an emergency and head back to Taif, but everyone would want to know what the emergency was. It would be embarrassing to explain my situation over the radio, but continuing the mission would be painful.

I decided I would declare an emergency and head back to the base. Just before keying the microphone, I wondered what all my bosses back at Beale would think if I declared an emergency. What would the bigwigs in DC think, since they would hear about it too? What would the UN think? I would probably get fired for aborting this mission, although getting fired at this point did not sound too bad.

It was no use; I knew I had to continue. I opened up the vent and tried to dry out my wet undergarments. Immediately, I became frozen and had to turn the vent off. With the vent off, I was warm, but my undergarments would not dry out. With the vent on, they would dry out, but I would freeze to death. It was a no-win situation. The Dragon was flying perfectly, but my suit had let me down. Who in their right mind would sign up for this crazy job, I wondered? This was not listed in the brochure.

I was miserable the entire flight. As I passed over Baghdad, I cussed myself out again. As I passed over Kirkuk, I yelled at myself some more. As I passed over Mosul, I cried a little bit.

After I landed, I never mentioned a word to the other U-2 pilots or my commander. I told the Supervisor of PSD, Technical Sergeant John Adams, of my predicament. He laughed and said they would take care of everything. The cost would be a case of beer. I was now laughing as we had no beer in Saudi Arabia, only near beer. I told him I would make things right.

I had known John since my early days at PSD. He was a very good friend. When I was younger, I was always short of money a few days before payday. John would always loan me a twenty to get me by. I never forgot his generosity. He was bailing me out again today.

***

In October, our military took a hit in Somalia when several Black Hawk helicopters went down, and vicious fighting ensued. The Pentagon tasked us to fly support missions for the Army in Somalia. I was up on the schedule to fly my longest mission yet, eleven and a half hours. It would take three hours to get to Somalia and then three hours to return.

The day before, I planned my mission and reviewed all my options in case something went wrong. There were few friendly countries between Taif and Somalia. Chuck and I decided if I had problems in the aircraft to head to Nairobi or Djibouti. Both places had a small contingency of Americans there. My biggest threat was from Yemen and their Surface to Air missiles on two islands I would fly over.

The night before, I made sure I got plenty of sleep. Takeoff was scheduled at sunrise with my return just before sunset.

The following day I woke up rested and ready to go. I got myself mentally prepared for this extended mission. As I lifted off, I turned the aircraft south and headed toward the Red Sea. I would not have an AWACS or RJ to talk to today. I would check in with the USS Lincoln aircraft carrier off the coast of Somalia when I arrived on-station.

The first part of the mission was smooth, as I spent most of my time sightseeing along the Red Sea. I had never flown in this part of the world before and only knew some of the countries from high school geography class. Two hours into the flight, I passed over the Yemen islands and their Russian-built SA-2 surface-to-air missiles. I was pleasantly surprised the Yemenis did not light me up on their radars as I passed overhead.

The Dragon Lady turned to the left as I entered the Gulf of Aden. I could see Somali coming into view out my right window. My track today had me heading straight for the port of Bosaso, then to

Mogadishu, and finally to Kismayo in the southern part of Somalia. After Kismayo, I would retrace my track back to the north.

As I hit Bosaso, the U-2 did not turn south like it was supposed to. The Dragon Lady continued heading straight toward the middle of the Indian Ocean. Something was wrong. The plane should have turned right. I grabbed my map boards and confirmed the plane should be in a right turn. I checked the waypoints page on the navigation system to match them against my flight boards. My navigation points were all off. Oh crap, I muttered to myself. I deselected the Nav mode and turned the heading knob to the south so the U-2 would not be too far off track.

I then started to punch the new coordinates into the nav system. I was struggling because the tiny buttons were too hard to select with my spacesuit gloves. The large gloves covered several buttons, making it difficult to hit the right one. After a few tries, I finally got the correct coordinates in the navigation box. Once satisfied, I selected Nav mode again on the autopilot. The U-2 jinked a bit but was now heading in the right direction. I finally began to breathe again.

I checked the next coordinate. It was wrong too. What the heck was happening? Did the mission planner get the coordinates wrong? The mobile pilot should have checked the coordinates on his preflight.

I spent the next hour punching new coordinates into the navigation system, trying to stay one step ahead of the aircraft. It was a long hour, but eventually, I confirmed all the new coordinates were correct all the way back to Taif.

I then realized I had yet to check in with the USS Lincoln. I wondered if they thought something was wrong. I keyed up the radio and told them I was on station and would appreciate it if they monitored my frequency.

The voice replied, "Yep, no problem."

That was the response, short and sweet with no small talk. It was the only words I would hear on my long flight.

The Navy probably wondered what they were supposed to do if I did have a problem. I was sure they would not let me land the Dragon Lady on an aircraft carrier loaded with fighter jets. Landing the U-2 on the USS Kitty Hawk aircraft carrier years earlier was met with limited success.

If I had any problems in the southern part of Somalia, my plan was to head to Nairobi. Any problems in the northern part of Somalia, I would head out near the USS Lincoln and eject. An ejection at 5,000 feet would give me time to make a safe parachute landing in the water. I assumed the Navy helicopters would pick me up. That was my plan, at least.

I made two more tracks up and down Somalia before starting my long three-hour journey home. It had been a long day, and the sun was setting when I landed in Taif.

In the debrief, we had a long discussion on what went wrong with my coordinates in the navigation system. Everyone said they did their job, so we just chalked it up to Gremlins. The Somalia flight would be my longest flight in the U-2 program.

***

My last flight for this tour would be my fourteenth total flight over Iraq. Everything was fine as I approached the Iraqi border. The RJ was coming off station as they had been up for ten hours. The AWACS had just replaced them as I checked in before heading into Iraq.

Thirty minutes later, AWACS called me and said they had a problem with their radar and needed to head back to base. I asked them if they could stay in the area to monitor me since I was well into Iraq. AWACS stated their orders were to head back to base. Dang, I thought, what if something went wrong and I had to eject? Nobody would know what happened. Would the Iraqis see the AWACS aircraft heading south and try something stupid? The Iraqis had been causing us headaches for quite some time.

Just then, I heard a voice; "This is Deep Sea; we can stay on station with you the whole time."

I was ecstatic. I didn't know who Deep Sea was, but they sounded American. My best guess was they were a Navy E-2 Hawkeye surveillance aircraft patrolling below the 32nd parallel. I thanked them and continued my mission.

Five hours later, I was passing back across the 32nd and called up Deep Sea to thank them. They were still there. Wow, I thought. They were true to their word and stayed in contact with me the entire flight.

The next day, I tried to find out who Deep Sea was, but to no avail. Everybody I called did not have a Deep Sea call sign in their flight operations. My boss and I laughed as somebody mentioned that Deep Sea was probably an Iraqi asset.

****

As a Director of Operations, my job was to put out fires. I took great pride in fixing any problems my troops might have.

One evening before I went to bed, I got an angry call from a Saudi officer. He demanded I come down to the flight line as two Navy jets had just diverted into Taif. He continued yelling that the Navy jets could not stay and had to leave. I grabbed my radio and headed over to the base. Upon arriving, I saw two Navy A-6 Intruders on the ramp with their engines running and one mad Saudi officer waving his arms in the air.

The Saudi officer informed me at the top of his lungs that the jets had no authorization to land in Taif and needed to go somewhere else, or he would call the police. Getting in my car, I called the jets on the radio to inquire why they had landed in Taif. We had no American presence or support on the base except for our little contingency. The Navy pilots informed me that one aircraft had an unsafe gear indication. The aircraft carrier would not let them land on the carrier in case of a mishap so the Navy diverted them to Taif. The A-6 pilot stated they were about out of fuel and needed to shut down their engines or they would flame out. One way or another, their planes were not going anywhere.

I went into negotiator mode. I tried to convince the Saudi officer that the planes could not take off again because they did not have the fuel and would have to stay the night. The official got even more irate and started calling his boss. I could tell this was going to take some time. I knew if the jets ran out of fuel, we would need Navy maintenance to come and check out their engines.

A few minutes later, the Saudi officer came back, still yelling. It was no use; he was not going to budge. I looked him straight in the eye and told him if those jets went airborne, they would crash and kill the pilots. If that happened, the Prince would be mad as hell and come after him personally. I did not know if a Prince was in line to the throne or what, but it was all I could think at that moment. The Saudi officer now looked worried and got back on his phone to make another call. After a few minutes, he agreed to let them stay overnight, but they had to leave first thing in the morning.

Feeling victorious, I gave the cutoff sign to the Navy guys, and they shut down their engines. After securing their jets, I took them over to our compound. We had one spare trailer for any VIPs that might come visiting. I put the two Navy guys up and got them some food, as I remembered the Deep Sea aircraft helping me in my time of need. The next day, we got them fuel and sent them on their way.

***

On my last mobile in Taif, I launched my boss Chuck Wilson on a mission over Iraq. When Chuck returned, he was visibly upset. The intercepts were continuing. Some systems in the U-2 also needed to be updated.

After every mission, Chuck would send out an email, or "Cable" as we called them, to all the bigwigs around the US and Saudi Arabia. The cable would recap how the U-2 flight went that day and if there were any associated problems. Today, Chuck titled this cable "Where's the Beef," from an old Wendy's commercial years earlier.

Chuck was tired of all the games being played in the system, and we needed some updates to the Dragon Lady. Without the updated system, our pilots could be in jeopardy. Coming straight from the Pentagon to Taif, Chuck knew how the military system worked, and he just threw a grenade into the mix.

We left and went home after sending the cable. As the sun set in Taif, it was rising in the United States. The following morning our phone was ringing off the hook. I answered a couple of calls and told the individuals to hold as Chuck was talking to another VIP. All hell had broken loose in the US as some commanders viewed the cable as going outside of channels, and others viewed it as we weren't getting the equipment we needed to fly our missions.

I always admired Chuck. He loved his pilots. He always stood up for his troops and did his best to ensure they had everything they needed to operate in a safe environment.

We eventually got a "band-aid" to our systems, giving us some more protections.

***

A few days later, I jumped on an American C-130 and landed at Dhahran Air Base, Saudi Arabia. I was scheduled to catch a flight to Germany the next day. Chuck wanted me to go to New York and talk to Rolf Ekeus at the UN. Rolf represented the United Nations Special Commission on Iraq. My purpose was to see if Rolf could get the Iraqis to stop the intercepts on the U-2s. It was a shot in the dark, but we had nothing to lose.

Before leaving Saudi Arabia, I stayed in Khobar Towers at the military installation. Soon after I got checked into my room, I turned on the TV and saw a picture of a U-2 crash at Beale Air Force Base in

California. The news anchor said one pilot had died. Something had gone wrong and the aircraft was on fire near the runway. The Dragon had bit another pilot. I got on the phone and called back to Taif. Chuck informed me that Rich Schneider had died in the crash.

I was heartbroken. I had been Rich's mobile a few times in Korea, and our desks were right beside each other back home at Beale. I could only think of Rich's kids and his wife and how devastated they must be. When I drove by the school, I would see all five of their kids walking home. Four kids had red hair just like Rich, with the youngest having jet-black hair. Losing Rich was a tough loss for our community.

We would lose Captain "Hawk" Hawkins in RAF Fairford two years later in a crash. We lost Captain Randy Roby on a test flight a year after that. It seemed like our squadron gatherings were weddings and funerals. I had not prepared myself for all the friends I would lose in the U-2 program. It was a dangerous business. Sometimes we had to wrestle the Dragon, and sometimes we got to dance with the Lady.

***

A couple of days later, I touched down in New York City. It was the first time I had ever been to the big city. The US Ambassador's office had taken care of my reservations.

When I walked into Mr. Ekeus's office I saw he had U-2 pictures on every wall. He even had a model of the Dragon Lady on the edge of his desk. We talked for a while, and I informed him of the Iraqi jets intercepting us and asked if he could get them to stop. He was surprised, as this was the first he had heard of our problem. I surmised Mr. Ekeus was not on the long list of recipients receiving any of our cables. After some small talk, Rolf promised he would do what he could. I left his office hoping we might be able to get the intercepts stopped on future missions.

Later, I was taken to Ambassador Madeleine Albright's residence to meet her. One of her representatives guided me through the Waldorf

Astoria Hotel and up to the top floor. A guard greeted us as we stepped off of the elevator. Her residence consisted of many tiny rooms with the ability to get lost fast. The Ambassador was having a party for somebody when we showed up. I didn't know anybody nor did I care, as this was not my scene. I was a fish out of water in the political world.

Eventually, the rep introduced me to Mrs. Albright, and we chatted briefly. She wanted to know about the Shiites in the southern part of Iraq and what they were up to. I had no clue what she was talking about. I had not received any of those intelligence briefings for Iraq and assumed she thought I was somebody else. I was just a pilot trying to get some help. I decided not to bring up the intercepts since we were both on different pages. I just hoped Rolf could help us out. I never did hear if the intercepts stopped on future U-2 missions.

***

On my final deployment to the Kingdom, we moved our operations to Prince Sultan Air Base (PSAB). The base was located about 60 miles south of Riyadh in the middle of absolutely nowhere. There was nothing but sand dunes for as far as the eye could see. Taif was a paradise compared to PSAB. The temperatures would rise to 128 degrees during the daytime. At least I was here in July, the hottest month in Saudi. There was no relief whatsoever from the heat or the wind. When the wind blew, the sand followed. We had to keep the plane in the hangar as long as possible to protect it from the harsh elements. If we did not launch the Dragon Lady by 8 am, our navigation system would overheat before we got airborne. If that happened, we would be done for the day.

The food at the base chow hall was great, and they provided all the free water we could drink. French and German pilots sometimes would meet us for lunch to compare flying notes.

Rumor was that Osama bin Laden's dad built our housing complex. I could never confirm that. It was a great place to stay as it resembled a nice apartment complex. We had a large swimming pool and the troops barbecued hot dogs and hamburgers daily. It was not the steaks the military served in Vietnam, but we did not complain. After all, the military provided all the free water we could drink.

We even had a movie theater and a little store to buy needed toiletries. The military tried to make it as comfortable as possible, and I thought they did a great job with what they had to work with.

I was assigned as the Director of Operations again. Times had changed for flying the U-2. Now all US assets stayed below the 32nd parallel or above the 36th. Tensions were rising. Over the years, Saddam flexed his muscles more and more. Since the area was more unstable, we took a complete air support package with us on our flights.

We now had "Tabletop" meetings the day before our scheduled missions. If we did not attend the tabletop meeting, then we did not fly, plain and simple. I was scheduled to take off and fly up and down the 32nd parallel. I was briefed to check in with AWACS and informed that an RJ would also be on station if we needed them. My fighter cap was six F-15s that would patrol beneath me. The air refueling tankers remained in Saudi airspace, while the rest of the package would be over Iraq. When the F-15s needed gas, they would slip over the border, refuel, and then head back on station. The Navy also had assets in the Persian Gulf if needed.

The next morning, I could feel the heat as I stepped out of the PSD van. Even though I was in an air-conditioned spacesuit, the portable cooler was struggling.

The Dragon Lady was as beautiful as I had ever seen her. Plumes of evaporating air from her oxygen cylinders bellowed from her undercarriage. It was an ominous sight, as the heat waved back and forth on the top of her wing. The Dragon was hot and wanted to get airborne to cool down.

As PSD was strapping me in, aircraft were lined up to takeoff. First, the big heavies went airborne, followed by the fighters. I had never taken such a large support package with me before. I wondered if they knew something I didn't. Were the Iraqis after a U-2 or about ready to start something?

Once airborne, I checked in with AWACS. The picture was clear, and they responded. The radio was ablaze with chatter from all the US aircraft. If the Iraqis didn't know we were coming, they did now. Even on our secure radio channel people were talking over each other. Thank goodness I only had one point to check in with AWACS near the western edge of my orbit in Iraq.

Iraqi planes started to pop up as we headed in-country. They stayed well above the 32nd parallel, knowing our fighters were poised to go hunting. Maybe I would get to see a dogfight today. The fighter aircraft patrolled around 40,000 feet below me. I could see their contrails, but not the actual fighters themselves.

My flight was uneventful, but tensions were higher than I had ever seen them over the last seven years. Less than four years later, we would be at war again with Iraq.

***

Surrounding our hangar we had painted red lines that only the U-2 could cross over. The one exception was the mobile car, which could cross the red line too, but only when following a U-2. If anyone else crossed those red lines, security personnel watching close by would arrest them.

The next week I was in the mobile car following one of our pilots taxiing in. Once the U-2 was parked, I was surprised to see the security personnel following me with their lights on. Immediately, I stopped the car. With weapons drawn, security motioned for me to get out of the car and lie face down on the pavement. Not wanting to get shot, I complied. The concrete was on fire as I lay face down and spread eagle.

I tried to keep my hands off the hot concrete as the temperature was near 120 degrees.

I knew the security guard had made a mistake and was probably brand new. I assumed he had not read his operating instructions or had missed the part that allowed the mobile car to follow the aircraft.

My commander, Major Al Cobb, and the rest of the recovery crew were laughing their heads off in the distance. They knew the guard had made a mistake too. There was nothing to do but wait for security to figure out the situation. Everyone was enjoying the show at my expense.

Soon additional security personnel showed up in more vehicles. After a few minutes of conversation, the new guard was informed of his error and came over to apologize to me.

After the debrief, I grabbed some Cokes and water to take to the security guard in his shack. He continued to apologize, feeling bad about his mistake. I informed him I was glad that no harm was done. It was better to be cautious than to let a vehicle full of explosives get through our perimeter. That would have been devastating to our squadron. The security personnel rarely got any thanks for their hard work, but I was very appreciative of their service even on this day.

A few months later, I landed on my 20th mission over Iraq. I had seen many changes over the last seven years. It was time to come home.

Panama

Panama's scenery was completely different than Saudi Arabia's. Dense jungles replaced the sand. If pilots ejected in the jungle they might spend the rest of their lives in a tree. If they survived and made it to the ground, they were on the dinner plate for the local wildlife. Heck, the insects could eat you alive here.

I arrived in Panama to fnd my old roommate Chuck Cunningham and his wife Troy there to greet me. It was like the good old days in training when we were all together and having a blast.

Howard Air Force Base was just south of Panama City on the edge of the Panama Bay. We stayed in the quarters near the top of the hill by the officers club. My room backed right up to the jungle. Erie sounds would echo throughout the night outside my bathroom window. I was sure there were monsters out there. I had my air conditioner on full blast to help drown out the noises from the jungle. We all joked about the two-step snake. If you got bit, you only had two steps before death. You did not go into the jungle for any reason.

Panama also had a wild side to it, and not just with the wildlife. Armed security guards floated around the parking lots of McDonald's to ensure your car did not walk off. During indoctrination, we were informed not to follow too closely to the vehicle in front of us in case we needed a quick escape. Kidnappings were not uncommon in this part of the world, and Americans were prime targets.

The base runway sat at the bottom of the hill. When it rained, the runway would flood as rivers of water would flow down from the higher elevations. One time we had boxes floating out of our hangar after a torrential downfall. Even some of the runway lights would explode as the water came in contact with the electrical wires. Dealing with monsoon rains was just part of everyday life in the jungles of Panama.

On some occasions, slow-moving animals would provide us with entertainment. Tree sloths would come down every so often to cross a road. Traffic would have to stop while the slowest creature on the planet inched across the pavement. Sloths constantly tested our patience if we were in a hurry. Everything in Panama moved on island time even though we were not on an island.

Wednesday nights, karaoke would get cranked up at the officers club. None of us could carry a tune, but we always volunteered the newest U-2 pilots. One evening Captain John Guertin had just arrived in Panama, and we orchestrated a plan to volunteer him to sing. John was a quiet and shy individual, so we knew this was going to be good. We preselected the song "Mona Lisa" by Nat King Cole since no one else could sing it very well. The stage was set, as nearly everyone in the club was in on the prank.

John showed up at the club on cue, weary from his arrival a few hours earlier. A few regulars started the night trying to win the $500 first-place prize. We booed the regulars off the stage in anticipation of John.

After a nod from another pilot, we started yelling, "John..John..John." The crowd joined in as John shook his head back and forth, indicating there was no way he was going to get up on stage and sing. We kept up the loud roar, and finally, John relented. Walking up to the front of the stage he grabbed the microphone. Initially, John thought he could choose the song of his choice, but that was not going to happen.

The announcer asked the crowd, "What song should we have John sing?"

In unison, we all replied, "Mona Lisa."

At this point, John knew the joke was on him as he began to laugh. He was a sport and was going to play along anyway.

The Karaoke machine started playing Mona Lisa, and John began to sing along. He hit every note perfectly. The entire room was suddenly quiet and in awe. We couldn't believe what we were hearing. John was an amazing singer. We soon realized the joke was on us. John took home the $500 prize while grinning at us for the rest of the night.

The next day, John took us all to Lake Gatun for a day of fishing. He paid for everything with his winnings. We caught our limit and had a fish fry at our quarters that night. We could not stop laughing until the wee hours of the morning.

Our operations officer, Major Keith Gentile, liked to take naps during the afternoons on days we did not work. Sometimes, for unknown reasons, Keith would leave his door wide open while taking his nap. On one particular afternoon, we took four boxes of stovetop stuffing mix and started spreading the contents all along the parking lot and into Keith's room. A dozen local raccoon-like animals watched us with interest from the jungle. Kudamundis as they were called were friendly for the most part, but sometimes they would get aggressive if there was food involved.

Once all the boxes were empty, we brought our lawn chairs out to watch the spectacle.

Within a few minutes, Kudamundis were everywhere and shortly a feeding frenzy had begun. More and more of the furry animals came out of the jungle. Soon, they were battling each other for every morsel as ten of them went inside Keith's room.

The screams that came next were terrifying. I think even the nearby Jaguars were frightened. Kudamundis spilled out of Keith's doorway and scrambled into the jungle. We were laughing so hard, one of us broke a chair he was sitting in. Keith was a great sport and laughed it off. I was sure he would pay us back later. It was a memory we would all laugh about for years to come.

I prided myself in getting my wife a present from the locals if I could. In Panama, it was pearls. They were not the perfect round pearls like those from other parts of the world, but shaped like a small oval. I got a few beautiful pearl necklaces for my wife so she could give them to her friends. She always looked forward to me coming home with gifts in hand. It was the least I could do since she was running our household by herself.

***

Our primary mission in Panama was drug interdiction. We were there to support the US effort to slow down the amount of drugs entering our country. It seemed like a hopeless task, and in many cases it was. Unlike other missions around the world, we did not get any feedback from the Drug Enforcement Agency. We must have provided some good intelligence or we would have closed up shop and moved on.

Most of our concentration was on the country of Columbia and the Medellin Cartel. Their leader, Pablo Escobar, was high on the list of government officials to slow down or even capture if we could. One of my first flights was to fly down to Paraguay and back. This mission would consist of four hours down to Paraguay and four hours back to Panama. This was the first time I had flown this far south.

After launching, I settled into my routine of doing nothing and started sightseeing. Where the desert was sand dune after sand dune, South America was an endless jungle. Occasionally, I spotted a small town or a river snaking through the forest.

Passing over the Amazon River, I could see the mighty river empty its contents into the Atlantic Ocean. The Amazon was the centerpiece of the beautiful landscape below. Glancing through the periscope, I could swear the river contained snakes as large as telephone poles. I could not imagine being eaten by a snake.

The towering cumulus clouds in South America could reach up and touch a U-2. I had never seen thunder boomers venture above 60,000 feet before, but down here, they were higher. Once, I had to modify my track to avoid a buildup. This was the first and last time I would ever deviate from my track for the weather.

Reaching Paraguay, I was at the end of my orbit. I was glad to turn around and head back to Panama. I had seen enough of the jungles to last a lifetime. I wondered how the camera could pick up anything along my track. I assumed the electronic equipment was providing some information. I knew our government was trying to locate Pablo Escobar when he used his cell phone.

On the long way back home, I watched the clock in the cockpit count off the hours. By now, I was getting used to flying long missions. I would stare at the clock for an hour and then eat some food. Then I would stare at the clock for another hour and get a drink of water. U-2 pilots lived in a vegetable state of mind on these flights. I would slow my heart rate down and just chill out.

I was happy to complete my first mission. I prayed the next mission would be different, as I did not want to return to Paraguay.

***

My next mission was different. A week earlier, Hurricane Andrew had hit Florida and Louisiana. The detachment was tasked to fly a camera mission for the Federal Emergency Management Agency (FEMA). The bigwigs in the States decided to use the U-2s in Panama instead of California. From Panama, we could fly to Louisiana and then to Florida and return to Panama. The distance for the U-2s out of California was too great for a pilot to fly.

I was excited to return to the United States, even though I would not be able to land. At least I could see America from the air, providing some comfort.

Once airborne, I turned north and headed directly toward Louisiana. I was flying the same route the drug runners from South America were making. Like the drug runners, I would return to the same airport I took off from.

I skimmed along the Gulf of Mexico between Cancun and Havana. As I approached the US mainland, I called Houston Center on their high altitude frequency. I told them I was en route to Louisiana and then on to Florida. Center was surprised to hear my voice as they could not find my flight plan. The controllers wanted to know what aircraft, tail number, where I had taken off from, and where I was going to land. Somewhere in the conversation, Houston Center informed me their system was having trouble with my flight plan since I was not landing in the US. Getting frustrated, I gave them the phone number to FEMA and told them to work it out with that government agency. I was surprised at the confusion as this was our third photograph mission for Hurricane Andrew. The controllers should have had this figured out by now.

After flying over Louisiana, I headed east toward Florida. Houston Center finally informed me they got my flight plan fixed and I was cleared to continue on. The thought of the FAA scrambling fighters to intercept me did not cross my mind until later back in Panama.

There was not too much to see in damage over Louisiana, but when I passed over Florida, it resembled a war zone. The last time I saw such devastation was in Iraq. Andrew had destroyed large swaths of southern Florida. Many people had lost their homes and lives.

When I took my last pictures, the U-2 slowly turned west and headed back into the Gulf of Mexico. I could see Havana out the left side of my cockpit window. The last time a U-2 flew over Cuba, Major Rudy Anderson was shot down during the Cuban Missile Crisis. I was glad my flight track was well off the coast of Cuba, as I did not want to be a statistic.

***

On Major Keith Gentile's next mission, I was scheduled to be his mobile. Keith was scheduled for an orbit track over Columbia and Venezuela. After the launch, I returned to the squadron to wait for Keith's ops normal call so I could head to breakfast.

Passing through 50,000 feet, Keith called back and said the navigation box dumped all of his coordinates. Without the navigation system, Keith could not continue on his mission. Losing our navigation system happened every once in a while when flying over the equator. The temperature near 50,000 was the coldest in the world, reaching minus 80 degrees in some cases.

We both confirmed he would have to dump fuel while descending back to the base. Our plan was to refuel the plane, upload the navigation box again, and then re-launch the U-2. Keith was not happy as this would add an extra two hours to his already long day. We had no other options except to cancel the mission and nobody wanted to do that just yet.

Once Keith was down, we pulled him out of the cockpit but kept him on oxygen as he waited in the PSD van. An hour later, we were ready to re-launch the aircraft.

On the second go, everything was fine. The navigation box did not freeze up this time. I was exhausted and I wasn't even flying the plane. I could only imagine what Keith was going through. When he landed, he was a zombie. After every high flight, the pilot flying always got the next two days off to recover. We needed the time off as the U-2 took its toll on our bodies.

***

After finishing my tour, I was home for only three weeks before finding myself back in Panama. My wife was not a happy camper. Generally, I could expect to be home for at least two months to recuperate from my deployment. In this instance, I had to replace a sick crew member scheduled to go to Panama. It was just part of our job in the Air Force.

In early 1993, The Revolutionary Armed Forces of Columbia, or (FARC) as everyone called them, had just come across the border in Panama and kidnapped some American missionaries. FARC had taken their victims back across the border to Columbia. Along with our drug interdiction tasking, now we had tasking to try and find the Americans.

The drug smuggling business had also changed as we noticed fewer flights from South America heading north to the States. The cartels were now using speedboats. They probably knew we were closing in on their airplane operations, so they changed tactics. With fast boats, they could haul more drugs than an airplane could carry.

A few days later, I was airborne, crisscrossing Columbia trying to locate the missionaries on the first half of my flight. I'm sure the family members thought the US was not doing enough to help find the kidnapped victims. Because of the nature of our missions, it was not broadcast that we were actively looking for the kidnapped missionaries. We all knew it could have easily been our family members kidnapped.

The second half of my mission, I spent tracking the drug runners. Instead of heading north across the open Gulf, the drug boats would island-hop all the way up the Caribbean Sea. Now I was tasked to fly eastward to Trinidad and Tobago and then head north along the Lesser Antilles. Over Puerto Rico, I turned southwest and headed back to Panama. Chasing the drug boats were long missions, but the beautiful waters surrounding the islands were breathtaking.

By the end of that year, Pablo Escobar would be killed by the Columbian police. Sadly, the American missionaries were also killed, and soon afterward, Howard Air Force Base in Panama was shut down.

Cyprus

The Island of Cyprus was as beautiful as they come. Its rich history and picturesque beaches were unmatched.

The Turks and the Greeks battled for the island for many years until the United Nations brokered a deal to divide it in half in 1974. The "Green Line," as people called it, was similar to the DMZ in Korea. It separated both countries. In some spots, the green line is only a hundred yards wide. Bullet-ridden cars abandoned during the fighting in 1974 still sat untouched in the middle of the line. Guards from both countries keep constant watch for any intruders.

Mount Olympus towered over our base, Royal Air Force, Akrotiri. Flying out of the British base was a blast since the Brits did not work on the weekends, which meant neither did we. At the other detachments, the weekdays and weekends blended together since we worked almost every day. Cyprus was like a normal job where we only worked nine-to-five, Monday thru Friday.

On the drive up to Nicosia, the first unusual thing I noticed was all the iron rebar protruding from unfinished houses. In Cyprus, if your home was not completed, you didn't have to pay any property taxes. There were no incentives for homeowners to complete their houses. Why pay taxes when you do not have to?

The museums on the island are some of the oldest in the World. In Nicosia, the capital, some museums' antiquities started in 6,000 BC, with the latest section at 1,000 BC. I had never seen historical artifacts that date that far back in time.

The British would have formal dinners at the Officer's Club on special occasions. We all dressed up in our military tuxedos and were treated like royalty. The dining room would consist of eight rectangular tables with eight people facing each other across the table. During the first course, military personnel would move down the row in unison, turn and simultaneously serve all eight guests on that side of the table.

Then in unison, the servers would turn and head off to the kitchen for the next course. The professionalism and perfection were something to admire. The Brits did it right in the military. It was a special treat for us Americans.

After we devoured our food, the cook and all the servers would be invited out. We stood up and applauded everyone for their service. They all took great pride in making it a memorable time for us.

Then the fun would begin. The Brits would start a Rugby game in the middle of the Officers Club in their tuxedos. Americans were in awe as this would be completely off-limits at any US military installation. Buttons and sleeves were ripped from their tuxedos. Before too long, all the participants had bloody noses. The rules of Rugby baffled us foreigners, but we cheered them on anyway, with our backs against the walls. I am sure the local seamstress was busy for the next week. I would be honored to have any one of those Rugby players in combat with me. They did not know what it meant to lose, no matter the cost to replace their uniform or fix their noses.

Many nights we sat outside over a fire with the British Tornado pilots comparing life in the military. Eventually, some Brits would bring up Winston Churchill. The Brits thought he was the greatest military thinker there ever was. I agreed and informed them that Churchill was half-American since his mom came from the States. Churchill brought out the best in both of our countries. He had British wit and wisdom, along with the American gung-ho attitude. We had many laughs while sharing stories about our time on the island.

On the 4th of July in 1993, we held our annual Independence Day picnic at the beach. We invited all the Brits since they were our hosts, and they showed up in droves. Our detachment provided all the food and drink.

It was a time to get together and remember we were all on the same team. It was off-limits to say why we celebrated July 4th. I am sure the Brits knew the importance of this date to all the Americans.

On Sunday nights in the summer, the Brits would have a concert at the Kourion Ancient Amphitheater near the base. The amphitheater gave a spectacular view of the Mediterranean Sea. On most nights, the sound of Opera would be floating across the night sky. Everyone would bring their favorite wine, cheese, and crackers while listening to Pavarotti. Some nights we could even spot satellites racing across the clear skies. I surmised they were probably American satellites keeping an eye on all the players in the Middle East.

***

Since we were island time, it was a whole week before I launched on my first mission. I was excited to get airborne again but not about this particular mission. I was scheduled to orbit over the Mediterranean Sea the entire time.

I pushed up the throttle in the U-2 as all 17,500 pounds of thrust kicked in. On takeoff, you can hear and feel the power of the engine. The U-2 only produced about 400 pounds of thrust at altitude, just enough to keep the plane flying. At altitude, a pilot could not hear the engine. The only sound above 70,000 feet was my inhaling and exhaling from my helmet's oxygen regulators.

After taking off on runway 28 at Akrotiri, I settled into my orbit. I could see Alexandria and Cairo, Egypt, out my right window. I strained my eyes to see the pyramids, but I was just too high. The triangular-face shapes of the pyramids made it too hard to spot this high up.

Once heading eastbound, it was easy to spot Beirut as billowing smoke towered over the city the entire summer. Even though Beirut's civil war had ended in 1990, fighting still persisted. It would be hard to get lost in the Middle East as long as the smoke from Beirut was visible.

Nearing the fourth hour in my flight, I heard a distinct "clunk" from the Dragon. It was a new sound I had never heard before. I scanned the gauges but did not see anything out of the ordinary.

Airplanes usually start talking to you before things fall apart. Now, I turned all my concentration inside the cockpit.

A few minutes later, I heard the "clunk" again, but this time I saw the hydraulic pressure gauge twitch. The hydraulic pressure needle was still indicated in the green band, but I knew something was wrong with the aircraft. Then it happened again as the pressure needle dropped a little bit more.

I decided to be proactive and call operations to see what they thought the problem might be. I explained what I had heard to Major Kevin Riebsam, the Operations Officer. After a couple of communications back and forth, I thought I heard him say to recycle the speed brakes.

I recycled the speed brakes and watched the hydraulic pressure needle drop to halfway on the gauge. Yikes, I thought. It was a hydraulic issue. I radioed back to Kevin and told him what had happened.

Kevin responded, "I told you not to recycle the speed brakes." Oops, it was too late now as I chuckled.

We devised a game plan to end the mission early and land back at Akrotiri. In most military aircraft, losing all your hydraulics is a major emergency and may eventually lead to an ejection. This was not the case in the Dragon Lady, as cables and not hydraulics operated my flight controls. I would lose my flaps and spoilers, but that was no big deal. My biggest concern was getting my landing gear down.

One of the first items on our descent checklist was the landing gear, so I grabbed the handle and placed it in the down position. Surprisingly, the gear came down and locked, but my remaining hydraulic pressure was gone. The needle read zero.

The descent took almost 45 minutes from my cruising altitude as I set myself up on a ten-mile final for runway 10. I made the approach as flat as possible with idle power. The Dragon loved to fly, even in idle power. I had to do a few S turns on final approach to lose altitude.

As I crossed the threshold, Kevin began giving me altitude calls. I planned on using my emergency spoilers during the landing to help kill my airspeed. At three feet, I hit the emergency spoiler button as the large panels on the top of the wing sprang up into position. The airspeed immediately started to bleed off as the plane settled down 3,000 feet down the runway.

I eased on the emergency brakes as the U-2 came to a complete stop. I was ecstatic as the Dragon was pretty easy on me today. Our instructors always urged us to practice no-flap landings on our training sorties. Today, it paid off.

Maintenance brought up a ladder to help me exit the aircraft. We decided to tow the airplane back to the ramp due to the unknown nature of my hydraulic issue. It was the correct decision as maintenance pulled off a front panel and hydraulic fluid spilled all over the runway. A three-foot black hydraulic hose had split in two. The loss of hydraulic pressure was my only emergency in ten years of flying the U-2.

Kevin came over and asked me, "You cycled the speed brakes didn't you?"

"Yes, I did. I thought that was what you wanted me to do," I replied.

We both laughed at our miscommunication. It didn't matter. As soon as I would have put my gear down, I would have lost my hydraulics anyway.

I thought I might get an award or a trophy for the great handling of my emergency. Instead, my commander, Lt. Colonel Bruce Jinneman, gave me the three-foot hydraulic line as a souvenir. I hung it on the wall in my room for another pilot to enjoy.

***

On another flight, I was scheduled to return to Iraq to support Operation Northern Watch. Instead of flying up from the south as I had done in Saudi Arabia, I would fly down from Turkey to the northern part of Iraq. The Iraqi Air Force was still limited to staying below the 36th parallel.

This time I took off and headed northeast toward Adana, Turkey. The US and Turkey had always had a tumultuous relationship. The Kurds in northern Iraq were straddled between Saddam and Turkey and neither one liked them. Northern Watch tried to keep the peace. Iraq and Turkey had battled for this territory for centuries. Both countries acted like a couple of old dogs fighting over a bone that had long disappeared years earlier.

As I crossed into Turkey, I hugged the Syrian border. A call was broadcast on my secure channel informing me Syria was "sweeping" me with an SA-5 surface-to-air missile. The SA-5 was a nasty Russian-built missile with a kill ring of 120 miles. I was well inside that ring. So far the Syrians were only looking at me with their early warning radar instead of their target tracking radar. The target tracking radar was the next step to firing a missile.

I had no idea who provided that info, but I assumed it was an RJ out in the Mediterranean Sea. Either way, I was grateful and thanked them for the warning.

I glanced north one last time before entering Iraq. My two alternates located in Turkey in case I had an emergency were called Batman and Van. Both were far from Iraq and if I lost an engine, there was little hope for me gliding that far.

Crossing into Iraq, I flew an orbit pattern aligned with the 36th parallel. I knew we had American fighters below me in the same airspace. I knew my best man at my wedding, Captain Tom Ruggiero, was deployed to Turkey at that time. Tom flew the FB-111 Aardvark aircraft. It was a supersonic fighter bomber and mostly flew low-level bombing runs. If I knew Tom, he was supersonic and as low as he could go. He loved waking the Iraqis up with a sonic boom to let them know the US military was still on patrol. I am sure many glass windows were shattered after one of his missions.

The mission was uneventful, and so far the Iraqis were not trying any intercepts this far north. I landed back in Cyprus and was ready for a long weekend off to enjoy some of the scenery.

***

On another sortie, I was scheduled to fly a camera mission over the Golan Heights dividing Israel and Syria. These missions were pre-approved by both Israel and Syria. The US provided the photos to both countries to ensure the other was not massing an Army near their borders. After crossing the Golan Heights, I would turn south down to the Dead Sea and back out to the Mediterranean.

As the Dragon Lady turned eastward after takeoff, I sat back and enjoyed my last flight. The entire mission was only five and a half hours—a breeze compared to the long nine-hour orbit patterns.

The U-2 lined up on the town of Haifa in the northern part of Israel. Beirut was slightly off my left nose and still on fire. I glanced out my right window one last time to see Egypt. The Red Sea had a beautiful contrast against the light brown sand. I remembered snorkeling down there on my tours in Taif. Growing up in Kansas, who would have thought I would get to do something like this?

Flying over Israel was smooth and peaceful. Not even a peep from the Israeli Air Force could be heard on the radio. Ten minutes later, I was over the Golan Heights crossing into Syria. Immediately my defensive systems came alive as it showed four SA-2 surface-to-air missiles scanning me. I could feel that nervous twinge in my back climbing up my spine. Some young soldier was practicing his tracking skills on me. I did not think the Syrians would fire at me since they had approved the flights and wanted the photographs. I hoped the radar operator got the message that this was a pre-approved flight.

My heart was pounding as I only needed a few more minutes, and I would be out of the danger zone and heading south.

Finally, after Damascus passed underneath my nose, the airplane started to turn south, and the Syrian radars went off my screen. Relief, at last, I thought. Times like this, military pilots should get paid more.

In the turn south, I spotted a road coming from Damascus. My mind immediately recalled the Bible and how Paul was on a similar road when Jesus spoke to him. A feeling of euphoria came over me as to the historical significance of the entire area. For some reason, the history of mankind came alive to me at that moment in the Dragon Lady. I was getting a bird's eye view of all the locations in the Bible.

Tracing the road south, I could see the Sea of Galilee, the Dead Sea, and Jerusalem. Beyond Jerusalem were the Sinai Peninsula and the Red Sea. I was a small fish in a big ocean.

After landing, I had a renewed appreciation for the historical importance of the Middle East and all the lands I was flying over.

Airshows and Adventures

Airshows were a special perk for U-2 pilots. We got to take the Dragon Lady to the public and answer any questions they had; after all, they were paying our salaries. Orchestrating the U-2's journey across the country was more complex than for other aircraft, as we had to take an entire support crew. In addition to the pilot flying the Dragon Lady, maintenance, extra pilots, crew chiefs, and other specialists would all have to pile into a KC-135 tanker. We also had to take all the special equipment associated with the U-2 and even our own fuel.

The U-2 used a special fuel called Propellant Thermally Stable, or JPTS, as all the crews called it. The fuel was specially designed for the U-2 to operate in extremely cold climates at high altitudes. JPTS would be pumped into one of the fuel tanks in the KC-135. Upon arrival at our destination, the JPTS fuel would be offloaded and then uploaded to the U-2 so she could make the trip back home.

In most cases, the tanker would take off early while the U-2 would follow later, giving the support crew time to set up for the recovery. The mobile pilot would obtain a chase car with a radio, while PSD would get a van to accommodate the recovery of the pilot. Generally, it worked like clockwork, but sometimes we had to confiscate vehicles and do whatever it took to make it all run smoothly.

My first airshow was at McConnell Air Force Base in Wichita, Kansas, my home state. I was thrilled as my parents would get to see me fly the U-2. When I landed, they were there to greet me. I have to admit I got teary-eyed as they were the biggest encouragers in my life and always pushed me to achieve my dream of flying.

The best part of the airshows was the kids. They always asked the best questions and were excited to see all the military aircraft on the ramp. Unfortunately, due to the security of the U-2, we had to have a rope around the plane so no spectators could get close to the aircraft. We did our best to explain all the aspects of life flying the Dragon

Lady. Sometimes we would have a PSD or another pilot suit up in a spacesuit and walk around the plane answering questions. A pilot strolling around in a spacesuit always brought in a large crowd to the plane.

Sometimes we did airshows at Navy bases. I once commanded a large gaggle from California to Navy Oceana in Virginia. Being a commander of a group of fifty personnel for an airshow seems like an honor, but it was a pain in the butt. I was constantly putting out fires and ensuring the airshow went off smoothly. I soon realized it was much better not to be in charge and just be a regular pilot flying the Dragon Lady.

Many Navy personnel did not know the U-2 flew off the aircraft carrier USS Kitty Hawk in 1963. The Air Force installed a tailhook on the Dragon Lady with a switch in the cockpit to deploy it. Today, the tailhook has been removed, but the red-guarded switch is still in the cockpit.

***

Moving the U-2 from one continent to another was an even bigger challenge than airshows. Sometimes we had to exchange a U-2 from California to Korea. We had two flight tracks to get the plane to Korea. One track was to fly to Alaska, switch pilots, and then on to Korea. The other option was to fly to Hawaii, then to Guam, and then on to Korea. All the pilots wanted to go Island hopping instead of cold Arctic flying.

On one such occasion, Major Keith Gentile led a contingency of support personnel to exchange a plane in Korea. I was the mobile pilot as Keith flew the plane to Hickam Air Force Base in Hawaii, on the first leg. We recovered him and then spent two wonderful days in sunny Hawaii before moving the plane to Guam.

The flight to Guam was a long nine-hour mission. We started early in the morning to arrive at Andersen Air Force Base before nightfall.

Landing in Guam, we immediately had issues getting rooms for all of the troops.

Typhoon Paka had ripped through the Island of Guam and wiped out almost all of the quarters on the base. As luck would have it, the military put us all up in the Pacific Island Club resort. We were scheduled to be in Guam for two days, but for some reason, the U-2 was broken, and we ended up staying for four days. Nobody cared or seemed to inquire what the problem was with the aircraft. We were happy campers trying to enjoy island life.

The Pacific Island Club was the largest resort complex I had ever seen. The hotel had seven swimming pools, one so large they used it for windsurfing only. They even had a church in the middle of the resort. We were living the high life until the plane was fixed four days later.

It was my turn to fly the Dragon Lady to Korea. The flight was scheduled for six hours and would pass over the island of Okinawa, Japan on my way to Korea.

As I was walking to the plane in my spacesuit, a civilian contractor approached me. I assumed he was from one of the defense organizations supporting the U-2 program. He yelled, "Whatever you do, do not crash this airplane; it has a one-of-a-kind camera on the nose."

I had no idea who this guy was, but you don't tell a pilot something like that before he gets into the cockpit. I was a bit upset and would talk with Keith after I landed. Some defense contractor was more worried about his camera than me. The Air Force could buy a new camera, but what about me?

Once airborne, I headed toward Okinawa. I was excited to see the beautiful island again, as I had not been there since the summer of 1982. The turquoise water surrounding the Island was as beautiful as I remembered it. I wondered how much the scenery had changed since my great-uncle had fought on the Island as a young Marine during World War II.

As I started my descent into Korea, the weather began to deteriorate. The weather guy in Guam said it would be clear and a million. I set up for an instrument landing on runway 27. Once in the weather, my head started spinning as I had a little bit of vertigo. I tried to shake it off but to no avail. I kept thinking about that knucklehead in Guam telling me not to crash the plane. I concentrated with all my might on the gauges to re-cage my eyes. I had never had vertigo this bad in my entire flying career.

Finally, I gave up and informed the tower I needed more time for the approach and would do a 360. I heard the mobile pilot come up on the radio and ask if I was alright. I recognized the familiar voice of my old roommate, Chuck Cunningham. I informed him I was ok and needed a few more minutes before starting the approach. As I started a right-hand turn, I kept the turn radius tight since I was in a valley surrounded by mountains.

My vertigo subsided once I rolled out on final approach. I felt a lot better and knew I had made the right decision by giving myself a little more time. I re-focused on the instruments and landed with no issues.

On the ground, Chuck asked me why I did the 360. I told him about my vertigo along with what the contractor said to me in Guam. I was glad as both me and the plane were in one piece.

That night Chuck took us out for some Korean Bulgogi. A great time was to be had by all. Chuck and I reminisced about our time at Reese and Beale. Chuck had a distinctive laugh that was easily recognizable in a crowd.

A few years later, we would lose Chuck to cancer. It hit the small U-2 community very hard. Our hearts were sad for Troy and their four kids. I had lost a best friend, roommate, and fellow instructor.

A day later, we swapped out airplanes and headed back to Guam. Once again, we stayed in the Pacific Island Club for two nights before departing Guam for Hawaii. It was my turn to take the long nine-hour flight.

I was scheduled for a 4 pm takeoff with a landing at Hickam AFB in Hawaii around 9 am the next morning. I knew it was going to be a brutal all-nighter. I had tried to stay awake as long as I could the night before to prepare myself. Since we had crossed so many time zones in such a short period, my body's time clock was completely out of whack. I felt like a walking zombie.

I stared down the long 11,200-foot runway as I gritted my teeth and threw the coals to the fire. The runway was unique as the first half sloped downward while the second half sloped upward. This always caused some anxiety with pilots of heavy aircraft as they would speed down the first half of the runway, then their airspeed would stagnate for a few seconds on the upslope. Eventually, the power from their engines got the aircraft to rotate speed to lift off. The U-2 did not have this problem as I lifted off at 1700 feet and headed eastbound.

Soon after airborne, I could hear the KC-135 tanker and my support crew taking off. The tanker flew faster than me and would arrive an hour earlier. This enabled Keith to get the equipment ready to recover me.

Like the sand dunes of Saudi Arabia, the blue waves of the Pacific Ocean flowed to infinity. There was nothing but water as far as the eye could see. The thought of only having one engine on the U-2 was a little unnerving. I could not imagine spending several nights in the Pacific Ocean in my one-person life raft. I prayed the ole Dragon would not bite me this evening. Thankfully, it did not.

The night sky soon took over as the last rays of light disappeared behind me. I took my time eating some peaches and pears. There was no reason to rush. Soon, I spotted the tanker below. They were racing 100 mph faster than I was.

Somewhere south of Wake Island, I noticed a bright light out in front of me. The light was slightly above my altitude and seemed to be moving. At first, I thought it was another aircraft. I was sure there were no other U-2s in the area. The more I stared at the bright light, the more it moved toward me. I convinced myself that this bright object was closing the gap between us. Was this a UFO, I wondered? This was the first time I had seen a bright light like this on the horizon.

I called down to the tanker and asked them what they thought the bright light was. They quickly replied, "Jupiter."

I laughed at myself and felt like a complete fool for thinking it might be a UFO. I replied, "That's what I thought."

"Yeah, right," the tanker Captain responded. I could hear laughing in the background during his radio transmission. They must have known I was thinking it was a UFO.

Finally, the sun came up with two hours to go. I couldn't wait to get on the deck as I was exhausted. This was a painful flight, and I was ready to get some sleep.

On my descent into Hawaii, Keith asked me to slow down as they needed more time to set up. It was the last thing I wanted to hear as my body was struggling. My temper was rising to match my fatigue level. I reluctantly complied, as I could not land without Keith in the mobile car.

After the longest thirty minutes circling west of Hawaii, I landed. As I exited the plane, I could feel my body straining to move. I needed a bed soon, or I would fall down. This flight was one of the most challenging flights I have ever flown in the U-2.

The Dragon Lady was taking its toll on me and my body as I was nearing 39 years of age. It was time to call it a day, and let the younger pilots full of energy wrestle with the Dragon.

Retirement

On the 3rd of May in 2000, I woke up both excited and sad. It was my 39th birthday and I was going to retire today. I would also fly my last U-2 flight in the Dragon Lady after 20 long years in the Air Force.

My wife and I drove separately as my "fini" flight was an early morning launch. Most U-2 pilots, on their last flight, choose to fly a low sortie around the pattern for a few touch-and-goes. I decided to jump into the spacesuit for one last high flight to see the Terminator.

At the squadron, I was greeted with many high-fives from other U-2 pilots, some I had known and trained throughout the years. It was surreal walking through the squadron for the last time.

During pre-breathing in the spacesuit, numerous PSD personnel came up and congratulated me. Several were my old bosses, twenty years earlier. When I started at PSD, I was right out of high school and brand new to the Air Force. Now, I was flying on my last flight. It was hard not to get choked up in the suit. As a former PSD technician, I hoped I had represented all the enlisted troops faithfully.

Chills went up my spine as I pushed the throttle up one last time. Then I was off, skyward bound. The morning sky over Northern California was crystal clear. I couldn't have picked a better day for my last flight. I knew the view would be outstanding. I glanced down at the climb indicator pegged to its limit. I would never see a climb rate like that again.

Climbing above 70,000 feet, the Terminator appeared for the last time. I could see for hundreds of miles in all directions. The slight curvature of the earth was even visible. It was like a postcard. The Air Force had treated me very well, and this view alone on this day was worth twenty years of service. For a split second, I thought maybe I should stay in the Air Force a while longer.

The Dragon Lady had taken me all over the world and had brought me back safely each time. I knew that was not the case for all my friends.

I patted my hand softly on her dash and asked her to bring me home safely one more time.

The flight was a mere two and a half hours. A piece of cake compared to the brutal nine-hour missions that I flew overseas.

I lined up on runway 15 at Beale for the last time. I could see six or seven mobile cars out on the runway. I was sure my wife and our kids were in one of them. I slowed the U-2 down to landing speed and concentrated on making one final great landing. A perfect landing would be a going-away present. The mobile started making altitude calls as soon as I crossed the threshold. I waited patiently to stall the Dragon one last time. The aircraft got squirrely on me, and it came down with a "thud." Crap, I said out loud in my helmet. I wanted that perfect landing so badly, but the Dragon had other ideas. She reminded me who the boss was.

I was embarrassed as many people saw a mediocre landing from me on my last flight. There was nothing to do but laugh.

After taxiing the aircraft into the parking spot, I shut the engine down and waited for PSD to install my ejection pins. I descended the stairs and greeted my wife as someone popped the cork on a bottle of Champagne. The bubbles sprayed all over my suit, but I didn't care as I took my final bow. Before entering the PSD van, I looked at the Dragon Lady one last time. I could swear she was smiling at me with her giant albatross wings. I seriously thought about going over and kicking her tire for what she did to me on my last landing. I decided not to as she got me and it was a fair fight.

Once I finished showering, I put on my Class A uniform and proceeded to my retirement ceremony. My wife and our two sons joined me on stage. I started to get a little nervous as I had not practiced a speech. I had completely forgotten about that.

Major General Glen Shaffer had flown in to do my retirement. As my former boss at the Air Force Technical Applications Center, Glen was as smart as they come in the intelligence community. My

Base Commander, Brigadier General Kevin Chilton, was also there to present me with a letter from President Clinton. Kevin had flown on three space shuttle missions and we were proud to have him as a U-2 pilot.

My wife Sherri received a bouquet of flowers from the President. Sherri had to run our household when I was gone, nearly a third of my time in the Air Force. She should have gotten the Medal of Honor for all she had to put up with.

The ceremony was quick. I looked around the room, pointed to everybody, and thanked them since I couldn't remember half their names.

Twenty years ago, I started my career 90 feet away in the PSD building. After 20 years in the service, I had only made it 90 feet, but those 90 feet were a dream come true and a blast to experience.

During the cake ceremony, General Chilton cut my tie in half. It symbolized that I was done in the military and would not have to wear these ugly ties anymore. It was a tradition I didn't even know about until I saw the scissors.

Soon afterward, we grabbed some golf clubs and headed to the course. I was sure the Dragon could not reach me there.

Conclusion

I went on to fly in the airlines for the next twenty years. I retired on my 59th birthday and called it a day in the flying profession.

Sometimes I think back and would like to fly the Dragon Lady one more time, to see her roar to the heavens and skim the earth's atmosphere. If I had another flight, then I am sure I would want another one after that. The Dragon Lady was addictive. I fell in love with her as a young kid and was blessed to have spent the last half of my Air Force career flying her.

Today, over 1,000 people have soloed the U-2. I was solo number 559. Amazingly, the aircraft is nearly 70 years old, with very few pilots ever taking her controls. Of all the planes I have ever flown, the U-2 was the most challenging.

When I look back on my time in the U-2 program, I'm not really sure it was me flying the Dragon Lady. I think she was flying me around the world for the time of my life. She was a beautiful lady that I will never see again. It was a long way from the hog farm.

It's time to take off our spacesuits and relax. I hope you enjoyed the adventure.

About the Author

Major Don Pickinpaugh was a Lockheed U-2S Instructor Pilot at Beale Air Force Base in California. He was the Assistant Director of Operations for the 1st Reconnaissance Squadron. Major Pickinpaugh also served as a T-37 Instructor Pilot for four years at Reese Air Force Base, Texas. He has over 7,500 flying hours in U-2s, T-38s, T-37s, DC-8s, and A-300s. He is married to the former Sherri Juall of East Lansing, Michigan.